4th International Conference on Electrical Energy and Networks 2016 (ICEEN 2016)

MATEC Web of Conferences Volume 50 (2016)

Nice, France
18 - 19 February 2016

Editors:

Ilhan Kosalay
Elmar Bollin
Meixing Guo

ISBN: 978-1-5108-2214-6

Printed from e-media with permission by:

Curran Associates, Inc.
57 Morehouse Lane
Red Hook, NY 12571

Some format issues inherent in the e-media version may also appear in this print version.

Printed by Curran Associates, Inc. (2016)

For additional information, please contact EDP Sciences – Web of Conferences
at the address below.

EDP Sciences – Web of Conferences
17, Avenue du Hoggar
Parc d'Activité de Courtabœuf
BP 112
F-91944 Les Ulis Cedex A
France

Phone: +33 (0) 1 69 18 75 75
Fax: +33 (0) 1 69 28 84 91

contact-edps@webofconferences.org

Additional copies of this publication are available from:

Curran Associates, Inc.
57 Morehouse Lane
Red Hook, NY 12571 USA
Phone: 845-758-0400
Fax: 845-758-2633
Email: curran@proceedings.com
Web: www.proceedings.com

TABLE OF CONTENTS

APPLICATION OF BOND GRAPH MODELING FOR PHOTOVOLTAIC MODULE SIMULATION 1
Madi S., Kheldoun A.

DESIGN AND REALIZATION OF AVIONICS INTEGRATION SIMULATION SYSTEM BASED ON RTX 6
Wang Liang, Li Bo, Tang Hengxian

ANALYSIS OF THE IMPACT OF URBAN MICROCLIMATE ON AIR CONDITIONING LOAD CONTROL 10
Hu Xiaoqing, Wang Beibei, Ji Wenlu, Shen Peifeng, Chen Peng

EXPERIMENTAL INVESTIGATION OF THE CORONA DISCHARGE IN ELECTRICAL TRANSMISSION DUE TO AC/DC ELECTRIC FIELDS 17
Fuangpian Phanupong, Zafar Taimoor, Ruankorn Sayan, Suwanasri Thanapong

DC-LINK VOLTAGE CONTROL TO COMPENSATE VOLTAGE DEVIATION FOR PV–BESSS INTEGRATED SYSTEM IN LOW-VOLTAGE (LV) NETWORKS 22
Lee Gyu-sub, Kim Yun-su, Chang Jae-won, Moon Seung-il

ENERGY COST SAVING STRATEGIES IN DISTRIBUTED POWER NETWORKS 26
Tcheukam Alain, Tembine Hamidou

MECHANICAL CALCULATION OF POWER LINES AND STRANDS IN OVERHEAD TRANSMISSION LINES 31
Li Yongping, Liu Yu, Zhang Jibin

A SIMPLE SHORT CIRCUIT ANALYSIS FOR POWER NETWORKS 35
Kosalay Ilhan

Author Index

Aims & scope

MATEC Web of Conferences is an open-access journal devoted to the publishing of conference proceedings dealing with Materials science, Engineering and Chemistry.

The journal aims to make conference proceedings visible, citable and widely usable by the scientific community. It offers outstanding services for the publication and dissemination of contents in order to ensure long-term archiving and maximum exposure of scientific events.

Coverage includes all engineering disciplines: civil, naval, mechanical, chemical, and electrical engineering as well as nanotechnology and metrology. The journal also deals with the physical-chemical characterization of materials, their implementation, their resistance in their environment, etc. Others subdisciplines of chemistry, such as analytical chemistry, petrochemistry, organic chemistry, etc., and even pharmacology, are also welcome.

Why publish with MATEC Web of Conferences?

- **Open access:** conference papers available worldwide.
- **Fast publication:** less than 3 months.
- **Total flexibility:** no page restrictions, free unlimited use of colour in the online version, any kind of scientific document welcomed (traditional articles, posters, abstracts and slideshows).
- **High visibility:** all documents indexed in main databases and easily found online.
- **Fair author rights:** CC-BY Creative Commons license.
- **Range of additional publishing options:** printed proceedings, CD-ROMs, copy-editing, etc.

Contact: Isaline Augusto
matec@webofconferences.org

ISSN (electronic edition): 2261-236X

www.matec-conferences.org

edp open Open Access Publishing from EDP Sciences

Preface

2016 4th International Conference on Electrical Energy and Networks (ICEEN 2016) was held in Nice, France during February 18-19, 2016.

The conference provides a platform to discuss Electrical Energy and Networks etc. with participants from all over the world, both from academia and from industry. Its success is reflected in the papers received, with participants coming from several countries, allowing a real multinational multicultural exchange of experiences and ideas.

Every submission has been peer reviewed by 2-3 reviewers in the right area, and more than 42 submissions have been received with only 17 of them were accepted for final presentation, in which 8 will be published in conference proceedings and the other 9 will be recommended to the journal.

This conference can only succeed as a team effort, so the editors want to thank the international scientific committees and the reviewers for their excellent work in reviewing the papers as well as their invaluable input and advice. Thanks also goes to the Guizhou University, China, International Association of Computer Science & Information Technology, and EDP Sciences for their various support to ICEEN 2016.

Prof. Meixing Guo
On behalf of the organizing Committees

Committees

Conference Chairs

Prof. Elmar Bollin, Offenburg University of Applied Sciences, Germany
Dr. Meixing Guo, Guizhou University, China

Program Committee Chairs

Assoc. Prof. Dr. İlhan Koşalay, Ankara University, Turkey

Technical Committee

Dr. Yacine DJEGHADER, Souk Ahras University, Algeria
Prof. Md. Mosaddequr Rahman from BRAC University, Bangladesh
Prof. Chellali BENACHAIBA, Bechar University, Algeria
Dr. Yingkui Yang, University of Southern Denmark, Denmark
Dr. Alain Tcheukam Siwe, IMT Institute for Advanced Studies Lucca, Italy
Dr. Hamidou Tembine, NYU, United Arab Emirates
Dr. Wang Liang, UAV Northwestern Polytechnic University, China
Assoc. Prof. Dr. Aissa Kheldoun, university of boumerdes algeria, Algeria
Prof. Benalia Atallah, Amar Telidji University, Algeria
Prof. Jin-Song KANG,Tongji University,China
Prof. Feng Shiwei Beijing University of Technology, China
Prof. Magdi S. Mahmoud, King Fahd University of Petroleum and Minerals, Saudi Arabia
Dr. Adel Abd Elbaset Mohammed, Minia University, Egypt
Dr. Lisnianski Anatoly, The Israel Electric Corporation Ltd, Israel
Prof. Mochamad Ashari, Telkom University, Indonesia
Dr. Riad Toufouti, University of Souk ahras ALGERIA, Algeria
Dr. P. Kanakasabapathy, Amrita University, India
Dr. Maryam Khanbaghi, Santa Clara University, USA

edp sciences

MATEC Web of Conferences

Statement of Peer review

In submitting conference proceedings to MATEC Web of Conferences, I certify to the Publisher that I adhere to the **Policy on Publishing Integrity** of the journal in order to safeguard good scientific practice in publishing.

1. All articles have been subjected to peer review administered by the proceedings editors.
2. Reviews have been conducted by expert referees, who have been requested to provide unbiased and constructive comments aimed, whenever possible, at improving the work.
3. Proceedings editors have taken all reasonable steps to ensure the quality of the materials they publish and their decision to accept or reject a paper for publication has been based only on the merits of the work and the relevance to the journal.

Title, date and place of the conference February 18-19, 2016 Nice, France

2016 4th International Conference on Electrical Energy and Networks (ICEEN 2016)

Proceedings editor(s):

Prof. Ilhan Kosalay, Ankara University, Turkey

Prof. Elmar Bollin, Offenburg University of Applied Sciences, Germany

Prof. Meixing Guo, Guizhou University, China

Date and editor's signature

17, avenue du Hoggar - PA de Courtabœuf – BP 112 - 91944 Les Ulis Cedex A (France)
Tél. : 33 (0)1 69 18 75 75 - Fax : 33(0)1 69 07 45 17 – www.edpsciences.org

MATEC Web of Conferences **50**, 01001 (2016)
DOI: 10.1051/matecconf/20165001001

Application of Bond Graph Modeling for Photovoltaic Module Simulation

S. MADI[1,2], and A. Kheldoun[2]

[1]University Akli Mohand Oulhadj, Bouira, Algeria
[2]Institute of Electrical and Electronic Engineering, Boumerdes, Algeria

Abstract. In this paper, photovoltaic generator is represented using the bond-graph methodology. Starting from the equivalent circuit the bond graph and the block diagram of the photovoltaic generator have been derived. Upon applying bond graph elements and rules a mathematical model of the photovoltaic generator is obtained. Simulation results of this obtained model using real recorded data (irradiation and temperature) at the Renewable Energies Development Centre in Bouzaréah – Algeria are obtained using MATLAB/SMULINK software. The results have compared with datasheet of the photovoltaic generator for validation purposes.

1 Introduction

The The first law of thermodynamics states that energy cannot be created nor destroyed but simply transformed from one form to another [1], [2]. By modeling the flow of energy from one form to another, a methodology that describes systems in multiple energy domains is obtained. One such methodology is *bond graph* modeling.

Bond graph modeling is one of the powerful tools used for the systemic modeling since it considers the same generic elements for every physical domain [3], [4], [5], and [6]. Where, any dynamic systems can be modeled using the store energy elements (C or I elements) addition to dissipate energy elements (R element) with convert energy elements (transformers and gyrators elements) in addition to the elements that are used to represent external inputs such as source elements (either effort source or flow source) and common effort or common flow relations (that are 0 and 1 junction, respectively). In addition, the dependency between these different elements is recognized by the causal analysis. These elements with the causality provide many advantages to this technique. They make easy the modeling of multi-domain systems such as electrical systems, electromechanical systems, mechanical systems… [5]. Bond graph technique is an energetic representation based on the flow and the effort elements and it offers a compartmental analysis and syntheses using the causality propriety [4].

Photovoltaic generator is a source of finite energy with a non-linear current-voltage characteristic that is directly converts the solar radiation into electricity with no noise and no high temperatures and no pollution. The photovoltaic energy is renewable and inexhaustible, so that, it is more and more intensively used as energy sources in various applications. Moreover, the photovoltaic is a very flexible energy source, its power ranging from microwatts to megawatts. In addition, the photovoltaic modules have a very long lifetime [7], [8] and [9]. In the literature there exist several mathematical models that describe the functioning and the behavior of the photovoltaic generator under different weather conditions (irradiation and temperature) [8], [10], [11] and [12]. These models differentiate from each other by the procedure of the calculation, the accuracy and the number of participant parameters in the calculation of the current-voltage characteristic [8], [10]. The basic element of photovoltaic system is a solar cell which could be considered as a sensor of photon energy. Practically solar cells incorporate a PN junction in a semiconductor across which the photo-voltage is developed [7].

In Algeria, There is an installation located on the roof of Renewable Energies Development Centre "CDER" in Bouzaréah, Algiers uses the Isofoton 106Wp-12 photovoltaic module to produce the electricity into the SONELGAZ grid (public company) without storage device. Such central grid-connected PV systems have an installed power up to the MW range. With such central photovoltaic power stations it is possible to feed directly into the medium or high voltage grid [7].

Many studies have been done on the CDER's PV installation among of them: the authors in [13] proposed a comparative analysis between: PVsyst3 software specific to the conception of the photovoltaic systems and the PSpice software specific for the simulation of the electrical circuit. While, the authors in [10] proposed a mathematical model which directly links the operating electric power to the pump's output water flow rate. This model is based on the analysis of the experimental results carried out in the pumping test facility of Renewable Energies Development Centre. The authors in [14] presented a method that permits to determine the optimum size of battery bank and the PV array for autonomous PV-wind hybrid energy system. And in [8] they determined the electric, hydraulic performances and the costs of the systems of pumping available in the Algerian market. However, the modeling and the simulation of operation of the photovoltaic pumping systems were carried out while being based on the experimentation.

Our study is focused on the application of the bond graph methodology to the Isofoton 106Wp-12 PV module. Therefore, in this paper, the bond graph modeling is introduced and highlighted. In addition, an analytical study of photovoltaic generator installed on the Renewable Energies Development Centre in Algeria is investigated using bond graph approach under different weather conditions. The obtained bond graph mathematical model of the PV generator is compared with that obtained using Kirchhoff's law. A comparison between real data and that given in the datasheet is done.

2 Bond graph methodology

Bond graphs actually indicate the structure through which energy is exchanged [5]. It represents the power transfer within a system by using a series of connections called power bonds [1], [15]. It is a graphical language that constitutes an intermediate between the studied physical system and the mathematical formulation (transfer function or matrix, linear or non linear state equation) necessary for its model. With the ability to map the power flow across energy domain boundaries, and map the signal flow information across the same boundaries, is an indispensable aid in the user's quest to form cause and affect relationships within interdisciplinary systems.

The bond graph modeling utilizes nine basic elements or building blocks which may represent physical subsystems, components or phenomena in every energy domains. The elements are classified in three categories, the passive elements and the active elements and the elements of the junction. These elements in addition to the detectors are used to represents the phenomenon that connect the generalized variables. For more details of bond graph methodology see [3], [15], [16], and [17].

3 Photovoltaic generator

The photovoltaic panel results to the combining of photovoltaic cells in series or in parallel or in both series and parallel. Basically, photovoltaic cell is a P-N semiconductor junction that directly converts light energy into electricity. Figure 1 represents an equivalent electrical circuit of a single solar cell and its bond graph.

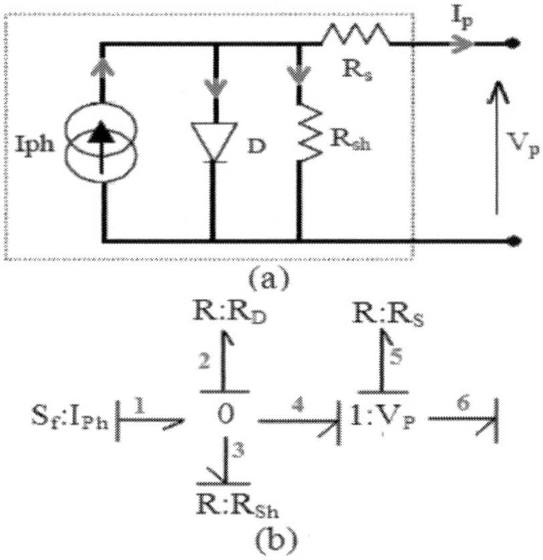

Fig. 1. (a) Equivalent electrical circuit and (b) its bond graph model of the photovoltaic cell.

This equivalent electrical circuit consists of a current source I_{ph} which depends on the solar radiation and on the temperature, a diode D on parallel in which the intensity of inverse saturation depends on the temperature, and the series resistance Rs which represents the material resistivity as well as the ohmic losses due to levels of contact. The shunt resistance R_{Sh} represents the cell leakage.

The bond graph representation of the photocurrent source (Iph) is a source flow Sf, while the shunt and series resistances both are represented by a resistance R_S and R_{Sh}, respectively. The diode (D) is represented by a resistance R_D, as shown in Fig. 1, (a). Using the assignments rules of the causality on the junction elements (0 and 1), the output of the block diagrame is the cell output voltage V_{Cell} that is represented by e_6 and given by (1). Using this equation, the obtained cell current given by (2) is similar to that used in [9], [11], [13], [14], [18], [19], [20], [21] and [22].

$$e_6 = V_{Th} \ln\left(\frac{I_{Ph} - \frac{R_S}{R_{Sh}} I_{cell} - \frac{1}{R_{Sh}} V_{cell} - I_{cell}}{I_{Sat}} + 1 \right) - R_S I_{cell} \quad (1)$$

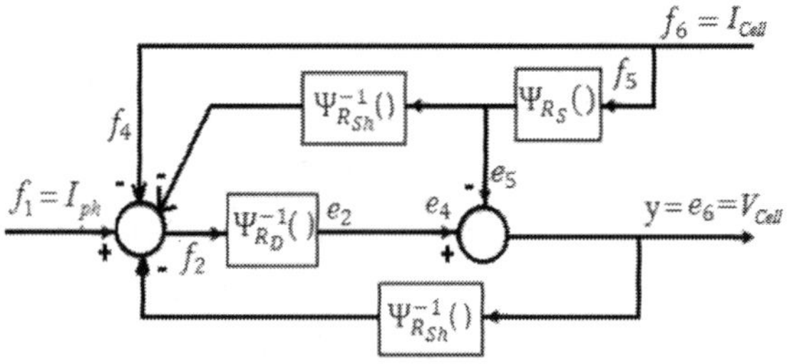

Fig. 2. The block diagram of Fig. 1.

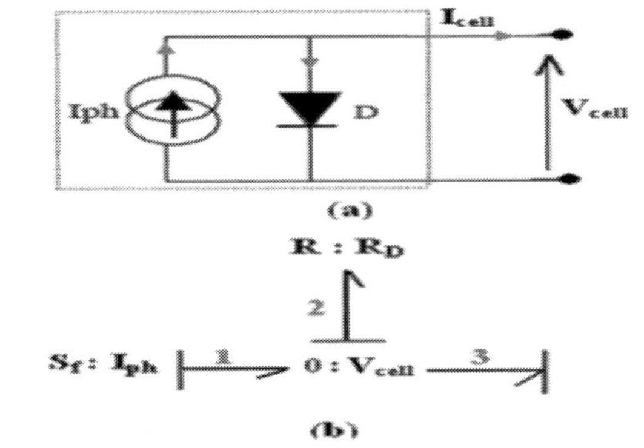

Fig. 3. (a) Equivalent electrical circuit and (b) its bond graph model of photovoltaic cell.

$$f_6 = I_{ph} - I_{sat}\left(\exp^{\frac{V_{cell}+R_S I_{cell}}{V_{Th}}} - 1\right) - \frac{V_{cell}+R_s I_{cell}}{R_{sh}} \quad (2)$$

with I_{ph} is the photo-current that is equal to the short-circuit current I_{SC}, I_{sat} is the reverse saturation current of the diode, V_{Th} is the thermal voltage.

Since the shunt resistance R_{sh} is very large and the serial resistance Rs is very small they can be removed from the circuit shown in Fig. 1 yields a simplified equivalent circuit as shown in Fig. 3 and its block diagram is shown in Fig. 4.

The output of the block diagrame of the bond graph model is the cell output voltage V_{Cell} that is represented by e_6. Using the characteristic equation of the junctions with the consideration of the causality results the cell output voltage V_{Cell}, represented by e_3, and the cell current I_{Cell} , represented by f_3, which are given by (3) and (4), respectively.

$$e_3 = V_{Th}\ln\left(\frac{I_{Ph} - I_{cell}}{I_{Sat}} + 1\right) \quad (3)$$

$$f_3 = I_{ph} - I_{sat}\left(e^{\frac{V_{cell}}{V_{Th}}} - 1\right) \quad (4)$$

This equation is used in [23] and [24].

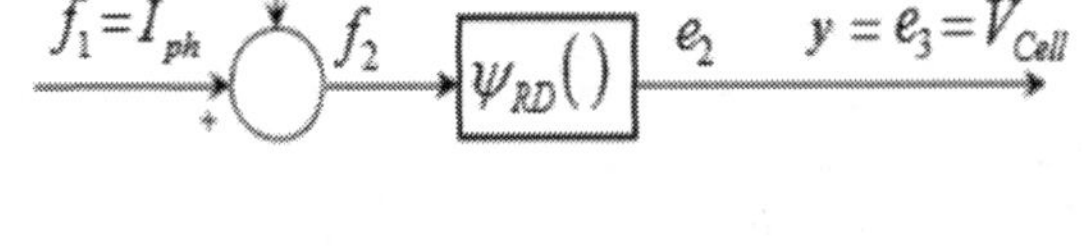

Fig. 4. Block diagram of the bond graph model of Fig. 3.

The two key parameters often used to characterize a photovoltaic cell are the short-circuit current and the open-circuit voltage which are provided by the manufacturer's data sheet [23]. Equation (4) indicates that the cell can be described by the relation linking the photo-current of cell to the reverse saturation current of the diode with the cell voltage. Figure 5 shows the output power and the V-I characteristics of the photovoltaic cell as a function of its voltage for Isofoton 106Wp-12 photovoltaic module at standard conditions.

For any connection of the cells the resulting mathematical model of the PV generator is given by (5 and 6). With V_{ThG} is the generator thermal voltage, I_{phG} is the generator PV current and I_{satG} is the generator saturation current.

$$I_{PVG} = I_{phG} - I_{satG}\left(e^{\frac{V_{PG}}{V_{ThG}}} - 1\right) \quad (5)$$

$$V_{PVG} = \left(V_{Th}N_S\right)\ln\left(\frac{N_p I_{ph} - I_{PVG} + N_p I_{sat}}{N_p I_{sat}}\right) \quad (6)$$

This equation is used in [21] and [25]. The output power of the of the photovoltaic generator is given by the following equation

$$P_{PVG} = I_{PVG}V_{PVG} \quad (7)$$

Consider the Isofoton 106Wp-12 photovoltaic module consisting of thirty six cells in series with two cells in parallel. Therefore, the total module output voltage is increased by 36 times the output voltage of a single cell while the module output current is the double of the single cell current.

Figure 6 shows the non-linear current-voltage characteristic of the photovoltaic panel under the standard climatic conditions.

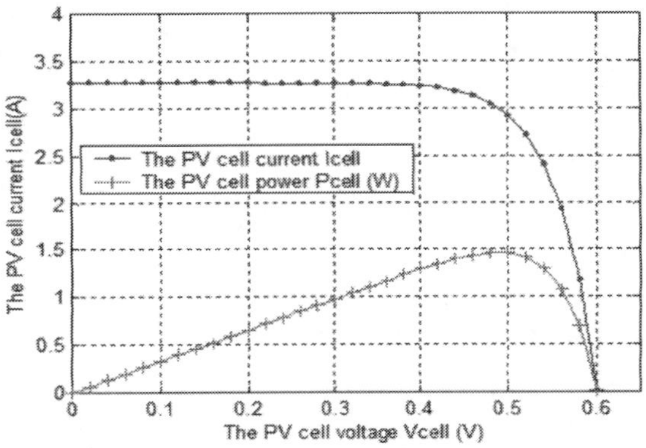

Fig.5. The V-I characteristics and the output power of photovoltaic cell as a function of its voltage V_{cell}.

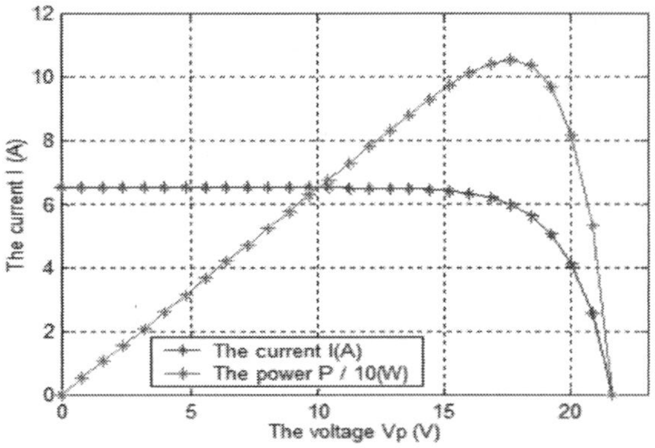

Fig. 6. The V-I characteristics and the output power of photovoltaic module as a function of its voltage Vcell.

A comparison between the Isofoton 106Wp-12 photovoltaic module parameters given in the data sheet and the results obtained using the previous equations with MATLAB software and real data, is given in table 1. This table shows that the obtained maximum output power of this PV module is 0.6234w less than the nominal power of Isofoton106Wp-12 PV module.

In other word, the obtained maximum output power of this PV module is 99.412% of its nominal output power which is given in the datasheet under the standard climatic conditions. Where, the corresponding PV module voltage is higher by 0.1950 V while the corresponding PV module current is lower by 0.1110A than that are mentioned in the data sheet.

Table 1. Comparison Between data sheet and the real data

	ISOFOTON 106Wv-12		
	Data sheet	simulation	Error
Maxim Power Pmax (W)	106	105.3762	0.6238
I_M at Pmax (A)	6,1	5.9845	0.1155
V_M at Pmax (V)	17,4	17.6083	0.2083

For different values of temperature and irradiation the non-linear current-voltage characteristic of the photovoltaic panel is shown in Fig.7. Where, as the irradiation and the temperature are higher the resulting output power of the photovoltaic panel is higher, but the nominal power of the photovoltaic panel is obtained under the standard climatic conditions.

4 Photovoltaic array

The photovoltaic array results to the combining of panels in series and/or parallel arrangements [6]. For practical application, considering the installation located on the roof of the Renewable Energies Development Centre in Bouzaréah-Algeria.

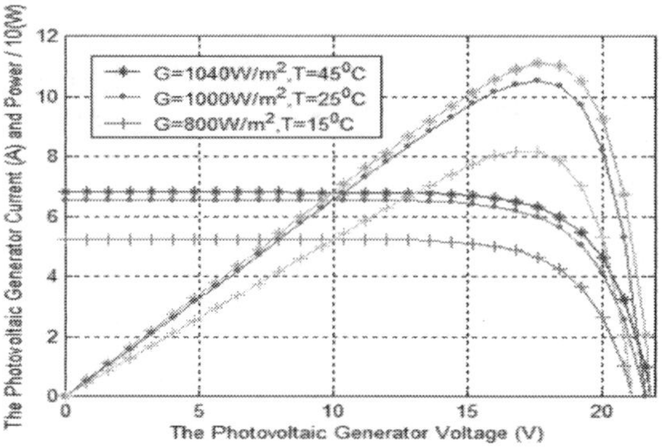

Fig.7. The I-V characteristic and the output power of the photovoltaic panel as a function of its voltage V_p.

In this installation the Isofoton 106Wp-12 photovoltaic module is used to produce the electricity into the SONELGAZ grid without storage device. This photovoltaic station that has a nominal power of 9.54 KW is composed of three sub-arrays. Where, each sub-array is consisting of two parallel strings of fifteen modules (Isofoton 106Wp-12) connected in series with nominal power equal to 3.18 KW.

Figure 8 shows the I-V characteristic and the output power of the photovoltaic sub-array as a function of its voltage. Where, the total sub-array output voltage is increased by fifteen times the output voltage of the single PV module while the sub-array output current is the double of the single PV module output current. The obtained maximum power of this PV sub-array is 18.7013W less than its nominal output power. In other word, the obtained maximum power of this PV sub-array is 99.412% of nominal power of this PV sub-array under the standard climatic conditions.

Note that those percentages are similar to that obtained for the PV module. By multiplying the maximum output power of this sub-array by the number of the sub-arrays used in this installation the total output power of this installation is obtained equal to 9.4839KW which is less than its nominal output power by 56.1W.

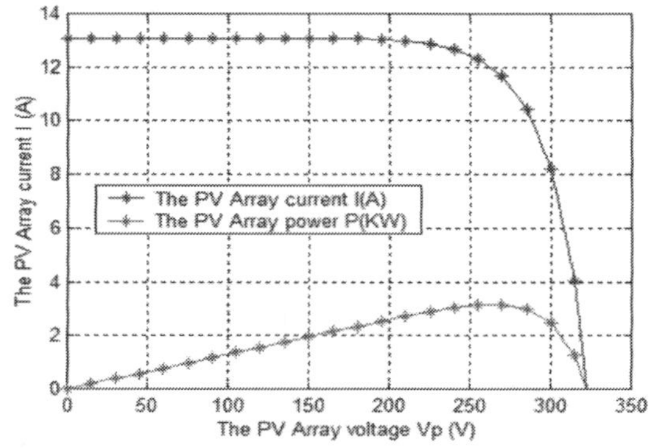

Fig.8. I-V characteristic and the output power of the photovoltaic array as a function of its voltage.

In other word, under the standard climatic conditions the obtained maximum out power of this PV array is 99.412% of its nominal output power. In addition, it is necessary to track the maximum power point all the time.

Where, several researches have been focused on the various Maximum Power Point tracking to lead the operating point of the photovoltaic generator to optimum point. Among of them: the constant voltage method, the perturbation and observation method and incremental conductance method [18], [25].

5 Conclusion

In this paper, bond graph approach has been applied to model photovoltaic generator. A real photovoltaic which is installed at the Renewable Energies Development Centre in Bouzaréah, Algiers and connected to the grid utility (SONELGAZ) has been the subject of the power modeling. Comparison of the obtained results with those mentioned in the datasheet of the photovoltaic generator has result to be in accuracy of 99.412%. Such modeling accuracy confirms the powerfulness of bond graph as a tool of modeling.

References

1. Y. A. Cengel and M. A. Boles, *Thermodynamics, An Engineering Approach*, 5th Edition
2. I. Dincer and M. Rosen, *Exergy, Energy, Environment and Sustainable Development*, June 2007.
3. G. Dauphin-Tanguy, *Les bond graphs*, 2000.
4. J. Belhadj, *Modeling, Control and Analyze of Multi-Machine Drive Systems sing Bond Graph Technique*, Electrical Systems 2-1, pp. 29-51, 2006.
5. L. Sass, *Symbolic Modeling of Electromechanical Multibody Systems*, UniversitéCatholique de Louvain, Electromechanical engineer Ph.D, 20 January 2004.
6. W. Borutzky and D. Margolis, *Bond Graph Modelling of Engineering Systems: Theory, Applications and Software Support*, Springer New York Dordrecht Heidelberg London, December 2010.
7. A. Goetzberger and V.U. Hoffmann, *Photovoltaic Solar Energy Generation*, Springer-Verlag Berlin Heidelberg, 2005.
8. A. Hamidat, A. Hadj Arab and M.T. Boukadoum1, *Performances et coûts des systèmes de pompage PV en Algérie*, Rev. Energ. Ren. Vol. 8, pp 157 – 166, 2005.
9. A. Zegaoui, M. Aillerie, P. Petit, J.P. Sawicki, A. Jaafar, C. Salame and J.P. Charles, *Comparison of Two Common Maximum Power Point Trackers by Simulating of PV Generators*, Published by Elsevier, Energy Procedia 6, pp 678–687, 2011.
10. A. Hamidat, B. Benyoucef and M.T. Boukadoum1, *New approach to determine the performances of the photovoltaic pumping system*, Revue des Energies Renouvelables ICRESD-07 Tlemcen, pp 101 – 107, 2007.
11. A. Talha, D. Beriber and M. S. Boucherit, *Performances of Photovoltaic Generator Multi-Level Cascade*, Jordan Journal of Mechanical and Industrial Engineering (JJMIE), Vol 4, N° 1, pp 163 – 168, Jan 2010.
12. D. Mezghani and A. Mami, *Input-Output Linearizing Control of Pumping Photovoltaic System: Tests and Measurements by Micro-Controller STM32*, International Journal of Advances in Engineering & Technology, Vol. 4, Issue 2, pp. 25-37, September 2012.
13. . A. Chouder, F. Cherfa, A. Hadj Arab, S. Silvestre and R. Oussaid, *Etude comparative de simulation entre PVsyst3 et PSpice de la centrale photovoltaïque connectée au réseau du CDER*, Revue des Energies Renouvelables CER'07, pp 131 – 136, 2007.
14. A. Kaabeche, M. Belhamel, R. Ibtiouen, S. Moussa and M. R. Benhaddadi, *Optimisation d'un système hybride (éolien – photovoltaïque) totalement autonome*, Revue des Energies Renouvelables, Vol. 9, N°3, pp 199 – 209, 2006.
15. J. A. Kypuros, *System Dynamics: Bond Graphs, Analaysis, and Control Design for Undergraduate Engineering Students*, 2008.
16. G. Dauphin-Tanguy, B. OuldBouamama, C. Sueur, A. Rahmani, *Les Bond Graphs pour: la modélisation, la commande et la surveillance*, Dossier realize par les professeurs de l'équipe MOCIS du laboratoire LAGIS, Mocis-Lagis.fr, 10/16/2011.
17. M. Roman, E. Bobasu, E. Iancu and D. Sendrescu, *On bond graph modelling of thermo-chemical processe*, ActaMontanisticaSlovacaRočník 15, číslo 1, pp. 33-37, 2010.
18. A. Chouder, S. Silvestre and A. Malek, *Simulation of photovoltaic grid connected inverter in case of grid-failure*, Revue des Energies Renouvelables, Vol. 9 N° 4, pp 285 – 296, 2006.
19. A. A. El Tayyan, *PV system behavior based on datasheet*, Journal of Electron Devices, Vol. 9, pp. 335-341, 2011..
20. N. Chandrasekaran, B. Ganeshprabu and K. Thyagarajah, *MATLAB Based Comparative Study of Photovoltaic Fed DC Motor and PMDC Motor Pumping System*, Asian Research Publishing Network (ARPN). ARPN Journal of Engineering and Applied Sciences, Vol. 7, N° 5, May 2012.
21. R. Singh and M. Pandit, *Controlling Output Voltage of Photovoltaic Cells using ANFIS and Interfacing it with Closed Loop Boost Converter*, International Journal of Current Engineering and Technology, Vol.3, N° 2, pp 417-423, June 2013.
22. P. Hersch, K. Zweibel, *Basic Photovoltaic Principles and Methods*, Published by Technical Information Office solar Energy Research Institute, SERI/SP-290-1448, 1982.
23. D. Rekioua and E. Matagne, *Optimization of Photovoltaic Power Systems, Modelization, Simulation and Control*, Green Energy and Technology, Springer-Verlag London Limited, 2012.
24. D. Mezghanni, R. Andoulsi, A. Mami, and G. Dauphin-Tanguy, *Bond graph modelling of a photovoltaic system feeding an induction motor-pump*, Published by Elsevier, Simulation Modelling Practice and Theory 15, pp: 1224-1268, 2007.
25. R. Faranda and S. Leva, *Energy comparison of MPPT techniques for PV Systems*, wseas transactions on power systems, Vol. 3, Issue 6, pp 446-455, June 2008.

MATEC Web of Conferences **50**, 01002 (2016)
DOI: 10.1051/matecconf/20165001002

Design and Realization of Avionics Integration Simulation System Based on RTX

Wang Liang[1], Li Bo[2] and Tang Hengxian[2]

[1]*National Key Laboratory of Science and Technology on UAV Northwestern Polytechnic University, 710065, Xi'an, China*
[2]*ASN Technology Group Co., 710065, Xi'an, China*

Abstract. Aircraft avionics system becoming more and more complicated, it is too hard to test and verify real avionics systems. A design and realization method of avionics integration simulation system based on RTX was brought forward to resolve the problem. In this simulation system, computer software and hardware resources were utilized entirely. All kinds of aircraft avionics system HIL (hardware-in-loop) simulations can be implemented in this platform. The simulation method provided the technical foundation of testing and verifying real avionics system. The research has recorded valuable data using the newly-developed method. The experiment results prove that the avionics integration simulation system was used well in some helicopter avionics HIL simulation experiment. The simulation experiment results provided the necessary judgment foundation for the helicopter real avionics system verification.

1 Introduction

With the development of science and technology, especially the increasing of computer performance, avionics systems play a more and more important role in the aircraft. Avionics systems have a crucial effect on the aircraft characteristics [1]. At present, with the improvement of aircraft characteristics, avionics systems become more and more complicated. It is too hard to perform the hardware-in-loop simulation experiment of avionics systems [2]. In this paper, a design and realization method of AISS (avionics integration simulation system) based on RTX is introduced to resolve the problem. Using this method, AISS design becomes very easy and AISS has a quite simple software and hardware structure.

RTX (Real-time Extension for Control of Windows) is developed by Ardence Inc. in USA. It is the only software solution designed as a high-performance extension to control Microsoft Windows. RTX is proven in thousands of demanding applications to provide enhanced performance, control, and scalability combined with unmatched dependability for industrial automation, military/aerospace, test and measurement equipment, robotics, and many other industries, all while reducing system costs and speeding time to market.

RTX is specifically designed as a real-time extension to the Windows operating system and is not an RTOS ported to Windows [3]. RTX provides precise control of IRQs, I/O, and memory to ensure that specified tasks execute with proper priority and 100% reliability. By operating in Ring 0 [4,5], RTX ensures the highest performance and requires minimal configuration, supporting sustained interrupt rates of 30 KHz with an average IST latency of less than one microsecond. What is more, the RTX Subsystem provides a high-performance TCP/UDP/IP networking for RTX applications. The RT-TCP/IP Stack supports Internet Protocol version 4 (IPv4) and next generation Internet Protocol version 6 (IPv6)[6].

2 Design of avionics simulation system

AISS is the crucial experiment system in the avionics system HIL simulation experiment [7]. The system can test and verify real avionics systems in the static environment of laboratory. The developers of avionics systems can modify the real avionics system by using the result of the AISS HIL simulation experiment. The typical AISS is divided into five parts: AIS (Avionics Integration Simulator), Pilot Control Stick, Power System, Ethernet Communication System and Signal Transformation Device. Figure 1 shows the whole avionics integration simulation system HIL experiment system structure.

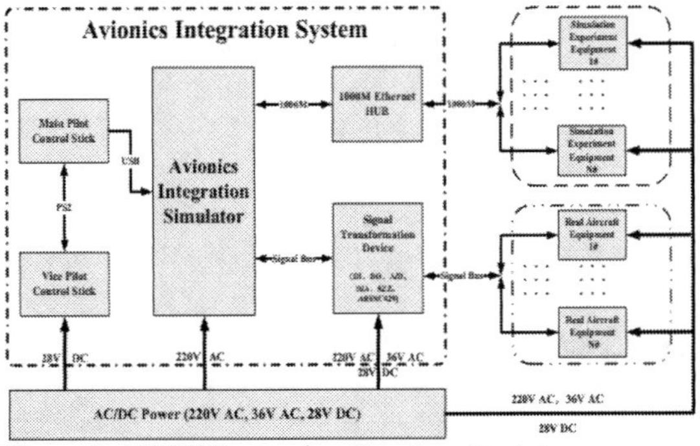

Figure 1. AISS HIL experiment system structure

AIS is the kernel of the AISS HIL experiment system. It can simulate all kinds of avionics tasks such as display of avionics system, data and message process, pilot manipulation, communication and so on [8,9].

Pilot Control Stick is connected with AIS by USB. Experiment operators can inject control commands into AIS by manipulating pilot control stick. AIS processes control commands, and then AIS sends messages to other experiment equipment by the signal transformation device and data cables (1553B, ARINC 429) [10]. Ultimately, it is implemented to simulate pilot manipulation by the pilot control stick.

Power System is used to offer all kinds of power sources such as 36V AC, 220V AC, 28V DC, 15V DC for the AISS HIL simulation experiment.

Ethernet Communication is used to swap data and messages between AISS and experiment equipment such as turn table, flight control simulator.

Signal Transformation Device is used to convert signals between AISS and real aircraft equipments.

2.1 AISS system software architecture

Hierarchical design is adopted in AISS system software programming. According to AISS different functions, AISS system software is divided into five parts: Interface Application, Real-time and Non-real-time Interactivity, RTX Application Dispatch, RTX Hardware Driver, Real Hardware.

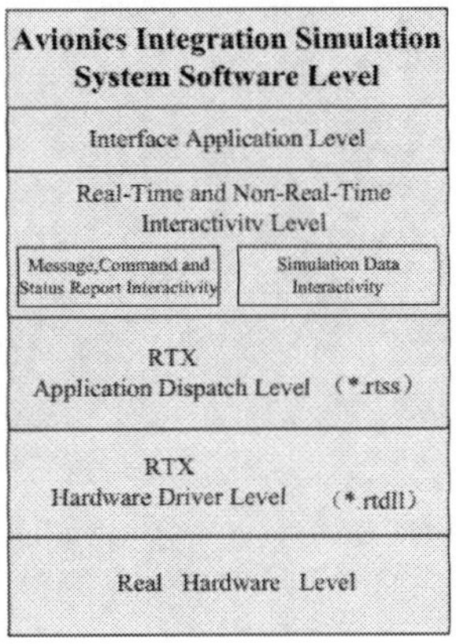

Figure 2. AISS system software levels

Interface Application Level is the level of human computer interaction control and messages display of AISS.

Real-time and Non-real-time Interactivity Level accomplishes the exchange of data and messages between the windows non-real-time application program and the RTX real-time application program [11,12]. According to different data and message characteristics, real-time and non-real-time interactivity level can be divided into two parts: simulation experiment data swap area, command and status report swap area.

RTX Application Dispatch Level masters the different real-time data acquirement, communication and process program running in order to meet simulation experiment needs.

RTX Hardware Driver Level manages and controls data acquirement and data communication hardware cards, including A/D, D/A, DI, DO, 1553B, ARINC 429, Ethernet and so on.

3 Realization of avionics integration simulation system

3.1 Realization of AISS open-loop characteristics

AISS open-loop characteristics mainly tests and verifies whether real aircraft equipments connected with AISS works well and their performance parameters meet the standard. In the AISS open-loop simulation experiment, functions of AISS include avionics signals simulation, fault injection, data storage, data analysis. In order to test and verify whether real aircraft equipments reach the standard, experiment operators can use AISS to inject faults into real aircraft equipments manually by building faults model in the AISS open-loop simulation experiment. Real-time and non-real-time mergence technique, virtual instruments technique and module technique are adopted in the development of AISS open-loop simulation software program. AISS is possessed of the realistic display, real-time response and stable and reliable data transmission by using these techniques.

3.2 Realization of AISS close-loop characteristics

AISS close-loop characteristics mainly tests and verifies whether avionics system design reaches the standard and has any design bugs and whether avionics system is reliable in the whole flight course. In the AISS close-loop simulation experiment, functions of AISS include avionics signals simulation, avionics messages display and monitoring on line, pilot manipulation simulation, sensors characteristics simulation, data storage, data analysis, flight character evaluation. Real-time and non-real-time mergence technique, virtual instruments technique, module technique and real-time Ethernet technique are used in the development of AISS close-loop simulation software program[13,14]. AISS is possessed of the realistic display, real-time response and real-time stable and reliable data transmission of network by using these techniques. Adopting RTX in windows operating system without any hardware timer, data transmission period of the avionics system can reach 1ms, the delay of AISS close-loop simulation can reach 5ms and the whole AISS close-loop simulation experiment period can reach 20ms in windows OS (operating system)[15,16].

3.3 Realization of AISS area navigation characteristics

Area navigation is one of the most important assessment standards in the avionics system verification. Area navigation is a flight capability that avionics system controls the aircraft to fly in the assigned area according to the track planned beforehand. Area navigation standard is that the errors between real track and planned track should be in a circle with R radius. R value is different in the light of different aircrafts. The flow diagram of AISS area navigation is shown as follows.

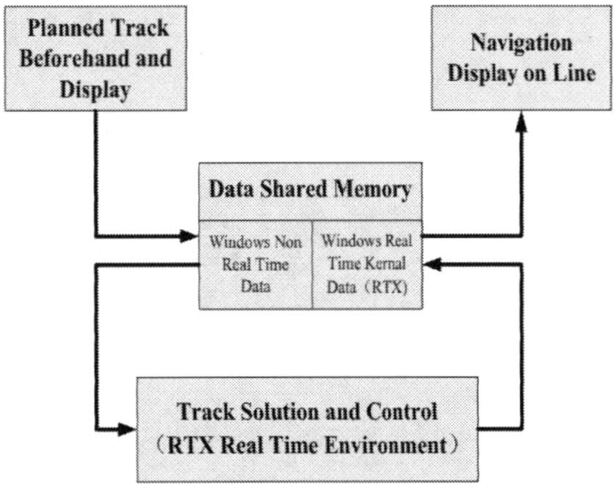

Figure 3. AISS area navigation flow diagram

In figure 3, AISS area navigation is composed of track planned beforehand and display, track solution and control, navigation display on line.

Track planned beforehand and display refer that route markings is installed and flight route is shown.

Track solution and control indicate that route markings planned beforehand are obtained from data shared memory (non-real-time data), then compute the control value on line according to (1), at last avionics system controls the aircraft to fly by the value of control.

$$0.00421 \times \phi + 0.128 \times v \times \delta = \sigma \qquad (1)$$

Φ (m): yaw distance, v (m/s): groundspeed, δ (radian): flight path angle, σ (radian): value of control.

Track solution must be the real-time computation, so the value of control should be computed in the RTX real-time environment [17,18]. At the same time, real track data should be written into data shared memory (real-time data).

Navigation display on line shows the real track obtained from data shared memory (real-time data) and the track planned beforehand. Comparing the real track and the track planned beforehand, experiment operators evaluate the navigation ability of the real avionics system.

4 AISS simulation experiment results

According to the method referred, AISS is used in the some helicopter avionics integration system hardware-in-loop simulation experiment. Some results of experiment are shown as follows.

4.1 AISS open-loop characteristics

The main items include SZZ output, A/D input errors, D/A output errors in this mode.

Table 1. AISS Open-loop HIL Experiment Result

Experiment Type	AISS Open-loop Experiment Result		
	Down-limit	Up-limit	Real Value
SZZ AC 36V signal	35.5 (V)	36.5 (V)	36.24 (V)
SZZ AC 1V signal	0.9 (V)	1.1 (V)	0.98 (V)
A/D input errors	-0.003	0.001	-0.0011
D/A output errors	-0.001	0.005	0.0023

SZZ is a kind of the sensor which can simulate the real aircraft sensor output [19]. In the table, the errors of A/D input and the errors of D/A output are asymmetrical errors.

4.2 AISS close-loop characteristics

AISS close-loop characteristics experiment result is shown as figure 4.

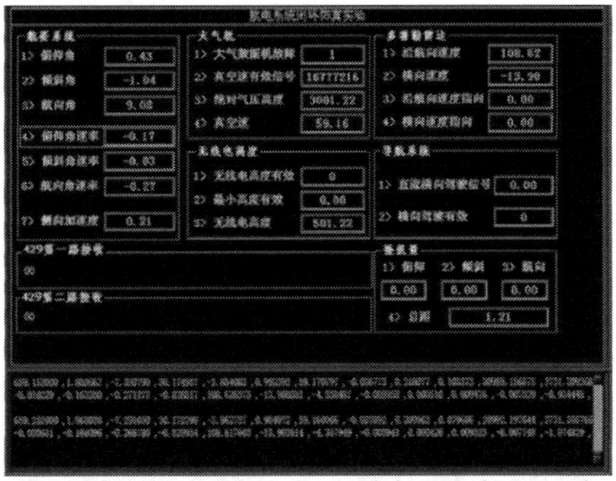

Figure 4. AISS close-loop characteristics experiment result

In figure 4, AISS can display all kinds of flight parameters on line in this mode. Meanwhile, experiment operators can simulate flight by manipulating pilot control stick. The flight parameter enclosed in figure 4 exceeds errors limit. AISS can alarm the flight parameter exceeding errors limit.

4.3 AISS area navigation characteristics

Figure 5 shows the result of AISS area navigation characteristics experiment. Points RA, RB, RC are route markings in figure 5. Broken line is the flight track planned beforehand. Aircraft flied by the RA-RB-RC route. Curve is the real flight track.

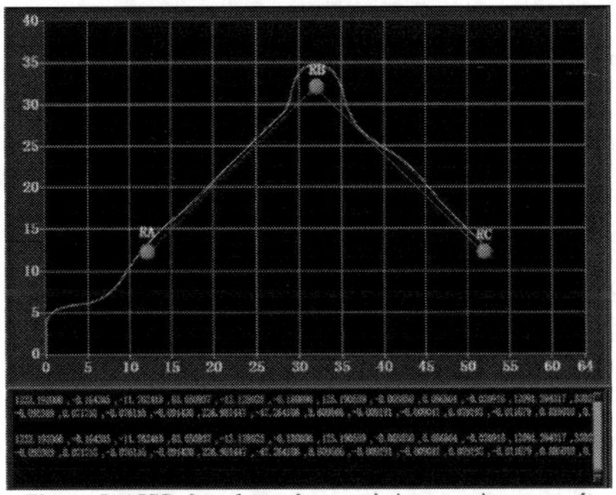

Figure 5. AISS close-loop characteristics experiment result

In figure 5, aircraft set up from point (0,0), then flied over RA. Aircraft switched the RA-RB route to the RB-RC route at a distance of 5km from the route marking RB. Ultimately aircraft landed in route marking RC.

5 Conclusions

The results of the experiment indicate that AISS based on RTX is adopted well in the helicopter hardware-in-loop simulation experiment. RTX is used in the AISS development, so AISS hardware has been reduced and AISS software is only developed in windows OS. The Special RTOS (real-time operating system) such as VxWorks is not used in AISS software [20]. Since RTX is applied in the development of AISS, it reduces the avionics integration simulation system costs and speeds time to the AISS application. Moreover, the development of AISS software becomes very easy and interface of AISS becomes quite friendly.

Using hierarchical design, it becomes quite simple that software developers debug, transplant, maintain and upgrade AISS software. If AISS software needs to be modified, software developers can just only modify some level rather than the whole AISS software. This promoted the software development efficiency highly and avoided the technology risk.

AISS based on RTX provides a good technology scheme and an implement method in different aircraft avionics system simulation experiments. What is more, AISS provides the technological foundation of testing and verifying real avionics system.

References

1. H.-G. Xiong, Z.-H. Wang. *Advanced Avionics Integration Techniques*, 1rd ed, National Defense Industry Press, pp.298-316 (2009)
2. X.-G. Song, X.-G. Zhang. *Fly-by-Wire Flight Control System*, 1rd ed, National Defense Industry Press, pp.97-131(2003)
3. P. A. Laplante *Real-time Systems Design and Analysis*,3rd ed., Wiley-IEEE Press, pp.1-19(2004)
4. D. A. Solomon and M. Russionovich *Inside Microsoft Windows 2000*, 3rd ed, Microsoft Press, pp. 20-69(2000)
5. Z. Dai, MATLAB software for GPS cycle-slip processing, GPS SOLUTIONS,16(2): 267-272 (2012)
6. Ardence Inc. RTX SDK Help Document.USA: Ardence Inc,(2008)
7. T. J. Farmer, T. M. McGruther. AIAA-89-3277 Flight Simulation Technologies Conference and Exhibit, August 14-16, Boston, pp.38-40(1989)
8. A. Cho, J. Kim, S. Lee, C. Kee, Wind Estimation and Airspeed Calibration using a UAV with a Single-Antenna GPS Receiver and Pitot Tube, Ieee T Aero Elec Sys, 47(1): 109-117 (2011)
9. T. Feng, HJP Timmermans, Transportation mode recognition using GPS and accelerometer data, Transport Res C-Emer, 37: 118-130 (2013)
10. M. Barczyk, A. F. Lynch, Integration of a Triaxial Magnetometer into a Helicopter UAV GPS-Aided INS, Ieee T Aero Elec Sys,48(4): 2947-2960(2012)
11. K. Harima, H. Saito, and T. Ebinuma, Navigation Message Decoding for Rocket-Borne GPS Receivers, Ieice T Commun, E95B(11): 3428-3431 (2012)
12. A. Hassan, J. Roth AIAA Paper 2003-3664, presented at the AIAA Applied Aerodynamics Conference, Orlando FL, June, pp.350-355(2003)
13. K. Salisbury, F. Conti Computer Graphics and Applications, pp. 24-32(2004)
14. A. E. Kirkpatrick and J. Sze, Proceedings of Eleventh Symposium on Haptic Interfaces for Virtual Environment and Teleoperator Systems, pp. 27-28 (2004)
15. J. Hu, Z. W. Li, Q. Sun, J. J. Zhu, X. L. Ding, Three-Dimensional Surface Displacements From InSAR and GPS Measurements With Variance Component Estimation, IEEE GEOSCIENCE AND REMOTE SENSING LETTERS, 9(4): 754-758 (2012)
16. Siddhartha Chib, Markov Chain Monte Carlo, Springer Berlin Heidelberg, 769(2011)
17. O. Montenbruck, P. Swatschina, M. Markgraf, S. Santandrea, J. Naudet, E. Tilmans, Precision spacecraft navigation using a low-cost GPS receiver, GPS SOLUTIONS, 16(4): 519-529 (2012)
18. M. Simandl, O. Straka, Functional sampling density design for particle filters, Signal Process,88(11): 2784-2789(2008)
19. D. Manwill, J. Blotter, R. West, A hybrid method for scanning laser registration using a general linear laser model, Mech Syst Signal Pr(2011)
20. G. G. Rigatos, Nonlinear Kalman Filters and Particle Filters for integrated navigation of unmanned aerial vehicles, Robot Auton Syst, 60(7): 978-995(2012)

MATEC Web of Conferences **50**, 01003 (2016)
DOI: 10.1051/matecconf/20165001003

Analysis of the Impact of Urban Microclimate on Air Conditioning Load Control

Xiaoqing Hu[1,a], Beibei Wang[1], Wenlu Ji[2], Peifeng Shen[2] and Peng Chen[3]

[1]*Department of Electrical Engineering, Southeast University, No. 2 Sipailou, Nanjing 210096, Jiangsu, China*
[2]*Nanjing power supply company, No. 1 Aoti street, Nanjing 210019, Jiangsu, China*
[3]*Rugao power supply company, No. 18 Zhongshan Road, Rugao 226500, Jiangsu, China*

Abstract. Due to the presence of urban heat island effect (UHIE), high humidity and other urban microclimate, temperature of city central area rises. This causes that the actual air-conditioning energy consumption (ACEC) in the urban central area is much higher than that in the suburbs. Load control of air-conditioners (ACs) is considered to be equivalent to a power plant of the same capacity, and it can greatly reduce the system pressure to peak load shift. In this paper, a simplified second order transfer function control model of ACs is presented, and its parameters will be influenced by the ambient temperature and urban microclimate. The temperature is obtained by using the temperature inversion algorithm of the heat island effect. Then, the heat index is calculated by combining temperature and humidity. The ambient temperature index of urban central area is modified based on the above microclimate, and the second order linear time invariant model of aggregated ACs is upgraded to the linear time varying model. Furthermore, the consequent parameter changes of the second order transfer function model are studied and the influence of urban microclimate on AC load control is analyzed. The proposed method is verified on numerical examples.
Keywords. Peak load shifting, urban microclimate, air conditioning, closed-loop control.

1 Introduction

Energy consumption is closely related to climate change [1]. There are obvious differences in the meteorological conditions of different regions in a city. The concept of microclimate is needed to characterize these independent meteorological conditions. Urban microclimate, represented by urban heat island effect, temperature and humidity effect, and cumulative effect, involves the climate characteristics between the near-ground atmosphere and the topsoil in a relatively small space. In the initial power load forecasting, when measuring the impact of the weather, only temperature was considered. Later it was found that the relative humidity, wind speed and cloud distribution will have a significant impact on the power load, especially relative humidity. Microclimate makes temperature of city central area rise, and causes that the actual air-conditioning energy consumption (ACEC) in the urban central area is much higher than that in the suburb.

During the hot summer days in a lot of cities, the energy consumed by air conditioner is 30-50% of the total electric power consumed, and this proportion even exceeds 50% in some central business districts [2]. Direct Load Control (DLC), which usually reduces the loads by controlling air conditioners of the residential users or the small-scale business users, is an important kind of incentive-based demand response. These kinds of loads have heat energy storage ability and can switch or change the control parameters in a short time. Such behavior will not cause obvious side effects on users. Meanwhile, they have the potential to balance system power [3]. Flexible loads can be incorporated into the normal operation of power system's dispatch by the demand response.

The impact of UHIE on ACEC has been widely studied. Ojima found that over the past decade, cooling load of the buildings in Tokyo has increased by 10% -20% on average due to the heat island effect [4]. According to this growth rate, it is expected to increase by more than 50% in 2030. M. stantamouris etc., pointed out that when the average heat island intensity of the Athens area is over 10℃, the cooling load of buildings will stiffen to double its original one in summer, and the peak load will treble [5][6]. By analyzing the simulation data of the outdoor air temperature of residential area, Li Xianting believes that the summer cooling load of urban residential quarters is increased by 10%-35%, affected by the heat island effect [7].

In most cases, the control scheme of TCLs is based on the idea of optimization. A scheduling decision model has an objective function to maximize the load aggregate interest and to minimize the actual output deviation of

[a] This work was supported by National Natural Science Foundation of China (71471036, 51277028) and S&T Foundation of State Grid Corporation of China (Key Technologies of District Power Grid Dispatch Considering Flexible Demand Side Resources.

ACs. It includes a constraint condition that the indoor temperature has to be within the range of [T_{min}, T_{max}] in order to ensure the user's comfort level [8][9]. In [10], the authors explored a simplified second order linear time invariant transfer function model by analyzing the duty cycle of the air conditioning group. They also proposed a closed-loop control strategy for air conditioners to be involved in direct load control. In order to achieve the desired control effect, the authors assumed that the outdoor temperature remains constant. This assumption makes the parameters of the transfer function control model remain unchanged. Based on this control model, further exploration is carried out in this paper.

In this paper, a simplified second order transfer function control model of ACs is presented, and an internal model control (IMC) algorithm is also used for aggregated air conditioning load control. The heat island intensity is obtained by using the temperature inversion algorithm of the heat island effect. Then, the heat index is calculated by combining temperature and humidity. Based on the above urban microclimate, the ambient temperature index of urban central area is modified, and the second order linear time invariant model of aggregated ACs is upgraded to the linear time varying model. The consequent parameter changes of the second order transfer function model are studied and the influence of urban microclimate on AC load control is analyzed.

2 Ambient temperature index modify based on urban microclimate

2.1 Temperature inversion algorithm of heat island effect

There are many limitations in the traditional methods of measuring the urban heat island effect, since they can not effectively study the characteristics of urban heat island from the perspective of space layout and internal structure. The development of modern remote sensing technology and geographic information systems provide the technical foundation to address these issues. Remote sensing information retrieval method is to carry out the surface temperature inversion by using the thermal infrared sensor, for the changes of the different wave band radiation values of urban targets. According to the radiative transfer equation, radiance of the entrance pupil of the satellite at a given wavelength location can be expressed as:

$$L_\lambda^{at-sensor} = [\varepsilon_\lambda B(\lambda, T_s) + (1-\varepsilon_\lambda) L_\lambda^{atm\downarrow}]\tau_\lambda + L_\lambda^{atm\uparrow} \quad (1)$$

where ε_λ is the surface emissivity, T is the inverse of the land surface temperature (LST), $L_\lambda^{atm\downarrow}$, $L_\lambda^{atm\uparrow}$ are respectively atmospheric radiation downstream and upstream radiation, τ_λ is total atmospheric transmittance. $B(\lambda, T_s)$, measured in $\mathrm{W\mu m^{-1}m^{-2}sr^{-1}}$, represents the emitted blackbody radiation when the temperature is T_s. $B(\lambda, T_s)$ is calculated as:

$$B(\lambda, T_s) = \frac{c_1\lambda^{-5}}{\exp\left(\frac{c_2}{\lambda T_s}\right) - 1} \quad (2)$$

where $c_1 = 1.19104\times10^8\,\mathrm{W\mu m^4 m^{-2} sr^{-1}}$, $c_2 = 1.43877\times10^8\,\mathrm{\mu mK}$. Based on the surface temperature inversion algorithm proposed by Jiménez-Muñoz and Sobrino11, the surface temperature can be approximated as:

$$T_s = \gamma(\lambda, T_0)\left\{\varepsilon_\lambda^{-1}[\phi_1(\lambda,\omega)L_\lambda^{at-sensor} + \phi_2(\lambda,\omega)] + \phi_3(\lambda,\omega)\right\} + \delta(\lambda, T_0) \quad (3)$$

where γ and δ are obtained by linear approximation of Plank equation. ϕ_1, ϕ_2 and ϕ_3 is the state equation of the atmosphere calculated from the atmospheric state parameters, and can be expressed as follows:

$$\gamma(\lambda, T_0) = \frac{1}{\beta(\lambda, T_0)},\quad \delta(\lambda, T_0) = -\frac{\alpha(\lambda, T_0)}{\beta(\lambda, T_0)} \quad (4)$$

$$\phi_1(\lambda,\omega) = \frac{1}{\tau(\lambda,\omega)}$$

$$\phi_2(\lambda,\omega) = -L^{atm\downarrow}(\lambda,\omega) - \frac{L^{atm\uparrow}(\lambda,\omega)}{\tau(\lambda,\omega)} \quad (5)$$

$$\phi_3(\lambda,\omega) = L^{atm\downarrow}(\lambda,\omega),\ \lambda_{eff} = \frac{\int_{\lambda_1}^{\lambda_2}\lambda f(\lambda)d\lambda}{\int_{\lambda_1}^{\lambda_2} f(\lambda)d\lambda}$$

Where λ_{eff} represents the effective wavelength of the sensor thermal infrared channel in $\mathrm{\mu m}$. $f(\lambda)$ is the spectral response function of the thermal infrared channel of the sensor. λ_1, λ_2 respectively indicate the start wavelength and the end wavelength, ω represents the atmospheric water vapor content in g/cm^2. In the above formula,

$$\alpha(\lambda, T_0) = B(\lambda, T_0)\left\{1 - \frac{c_2}{T_0}\left[\frac{\lambda^4}{c_1}B(\lambda, T_0) + \frac{1}{\lambda}\right]\right\} \quad (6)$$

$$\beta(\lambda, T_0) = \frac{c_2 B(\lambda, T_0)}{T_0^2}\left[\frac{\lambda^4}{c_1}B(\lambda, T_0) + \frac{1}{\lambda}\right] \quad (7)$$

2.2 The heat index calculated by combining temperature and humidity

Unlike air temperature which tells how warm or cool the actual air around us is, apparent temperature tells us how warm or cool our bodies perceive the air to be. When the human body overheats, it cools itself by perspiring, or sweating; heat is then removed from the body by evaporation of that sweat. Humidity, however, slows the rate of this evaporation. The more moisture the surrounding air contains, the less moisture it's able to absorb from the skin's surface through evaporation. With less evaporation occurring, less heat is removed from the body, which is the reason why the air feels hotter than it really is when it's humid outside.

The heat index is a measure of how hot it feels outdoors as a result of air temperature and relative humidity combined. The computation of the heat index is a refinement of a result obtained by multiple regression analysis carried out by Lans P. Rothfusz12.

$$\begin{aligned}\text{Heat Index} = &-42.379 + 2.04901523T + 10.14333127RH - 0.22475541TRH \\ &- 6.83783\times10^{-3}T^2 - 5.481717\times10^{-2}RH^2 + 1.22874\times10^{-3}T^2RH \\ &+ 8.5282\times10^{-4}TRH^2 - 1.99\times10^{-6}T^2RH^2\end{aligned} \quad (8)$$

where T is temperature in degrees F and RH is relative humidity in percent. HI is the heat index expressed as an apparent temperature in degrees F. If the RH is less than

13% and the temperature is between 80 and 112 degrees F, then the following adjustment is subtracted from *HI*:

$$\text{ADJUSTMENT}=[(13-RH)/4]*\sqrt{(17-|T-95.|)/17} \quad (9)$$

On the other hand, if the *RH* is greater than 85% and the temperature is between 80 and 87 degrees F, then the following adjustment is added to *HI*:

$$\text{ADJUSTMENT}=[(RH-85)/10]*[(87-T)/5] \quad (10)$$

The Rothfusz regression is not appropriate when conditions of temperature and humidity warrant a heat index value below about 80 degrees F. In those cases, a simpler formula is applied to calculate values consistent with Steadman's results:

$$HI=0.5*\{T+61.0+[(T-68.0)*1.2]+(RH*0.094)\} \quad (11)$$

In practice, the formula is computed first and the result averaged with the temperature. If this above heat index value is 80 degrees F or higher, the full regression equation along with any adjustment as described above is applied.

3 A transfer function model for the second order linear time invariant system

When the temperature set point rises 0.5 ℃, the response of a population consisting of n ACs will be:

$$D(t)=D_{ss}(\theta_{ref})+L^{-1}\left(G_p(s)0.5/s\right) \quad (12)$$

Where $D_{ss}(\theta_{ref})$ is the asymptotic mean steady-state aggregated power demand of the AC group with constant temperature set point. It is also the duty cycle of the steady state. The term including $G_p(s)$, which belongs to a transient process of change, indicates the aggregated demand response of a 0.5 ℃ step in the form of a second-order linear model.

$$D_{ss}(\theta)=\left(1+\frac{\log\left(1+\dfrac{H}{\theta_a-\theta-H/2}\right)}{\log\left(1+\dfrac{H}{PR-\theta_a+\theta-H/2}\right)}\right)^{-1} \quad (13)$$

Where the hysteresis width H is obtained by the upper and lower limit of temperature which determines whether the AC is operating or switched off:

$$H=\theta_{+}-\theta_{-} \quad (14)$$

The second order transfer function model of an AC group is:

$$G_p(s)=\frac{b_2s^2+b_1s+b_0}{s^2+2\xi\omega_n s+\omega_n^2} \quad (15)$$

Whose parameters are calculated from the equivalent thermal capacitance, thermal resistance, thermal power, hysteresis width and so on. The damping ratio ξ and the undamped natural oscillation ω_n of the characteristic polynomials in the denominator are:

$$\xi=\frac{\log(r)}{\sqrt{\pi^2+\log^2(r)}},\quad \omega_n=\frac{\pi\mu_v}{\sqrt{1-\xi^2}}, \quad (16)$$

The coefficients in the numerator are:

$$b_0=\frac{\omega_n^2\left(D_{ss}\left(\theta_{ref}+0.5\right)-D_{ss}(\theta_{ref})\right)}{0.5}, \quad (17)$$

$$b_1=0.5\mu_v+2b_2\xi\omega_n,\quad b_2=D_{ss}(\theta_{ref}), \quad (18)$$

μ_v represents the mean values of v

$$r=\frac{\left|\operatorname{erf}\left(\dfrac{1}{0.9+2\sqrt{2}\sigma_{rel}}\right)-0.5\right|}{\left|\operatorname{erf}\left(\dfrac{1}{0.9}\right)-0.5\right|} \quad (19)$$

where erf represents the Gaussian error function.

4 A load control strategy for the AC group via the IMC controller

Figure 1 shows a load control strategy for the AC group based on the internal model controller (IMC). The above second order transfer function model is used to design an IMC control structure to compute common offsets to a temperature set point to be broadcast to the ACs as a control signal.

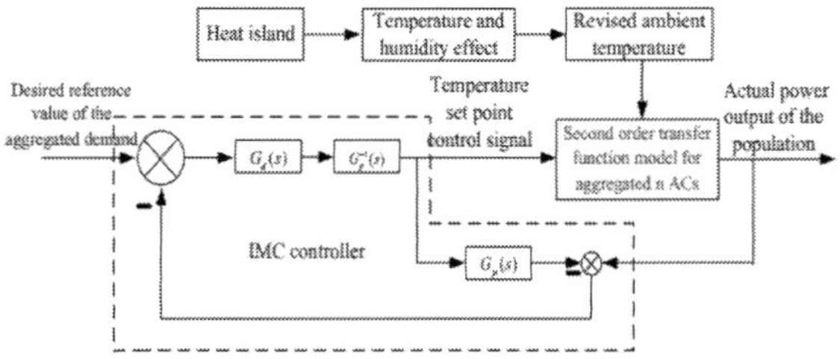

Figure 1. A load control strategy for the AC group via the IMC controller, according to the modified ambient temperature index based on the urban micro climate

The desired reference demand of the ACs minus the actual output power of them is the load tracking error, when the event of load control occurs. This load tracking error is taken as the input of the IMC controller. The heat island intensity is obtained by using the temperature inversion algorithm of the heat island effect. Then, the heat index is calculated by combining temperature and humidity. Based on the above microclimate, the ambient temperature index of urban central area is modified. From equations (12)- (19) it can be seen that, the parameters of the second order transfer function model for aggregated n ACs vary with the ambient temperature. Consequently, the second order linear time invariant model is upgraded to the linear time varying model. The calculated temperature set point $u(t)$ is considered as the control signal of the air conditioning group.

The IMC controller contains a model of the control plant $G_p(s)$, its inverse $G_p^{-1}(s)$, and the target desired behaviour in the closed loop represented by its transfer function $G_d(s)$. $G_p(s)$ is the second order transfer function model of an AC group. For simplicity, we propose a first-order inertial element:

$$G_d(s)=\frac{1}{T_c s+1} \quad (20)$$

Where T_c is the desired closed-loop time constant of the system. Because in air conditioning load control, reaching the steady state reference value within 10 min is reasonable, this paper chose $T_c=2$ min.

5 Case study: demand shaping performance

A population of ACs of similar characteristics can be regarded as a control group. We take a downtown area in Nanjing, China, as the research object where there are 18000 ACs of 10000 residents participating in the demand response plan. Parameters of ACs in the group are as follows: thermal resistance $R \sim LN(2, 0.4^2)$, thermal capacitance $C \sim LN(3.6, 0.72^2)$, thermal power $P \sim LN(6, 1.2^2)$. In this section, two scenario analytics by varying the temperature set point offset to control the aggregated power demand of ACs is carried out. Assuming that at the initial moment, 44.6% of the ACs are on, while the rest of them are off.

5.1 Scenario 1: AC load control without considering urban microclimate

In this scenario, the influence of urban microclimate on AC load control is neglected, and the parameters of the air conditioners remain unchanged, which are given in Table 1.

Table 1. Parameters of the air conditioners.

Parameters	Value	Description
R	μ_R = 2 °C/kW	Equivalent thermal resistance, log-normally distributed with mean μ_R and variance
C	μ_C = 3.6 kWh/°C	Equivalent heat capacity log-normally distributed with mean μ_C and variance σ_C^2
P	μ_P = 6 kW	Equivalent thermal power, log-normally distributed with mean μ_P and variance σ_P^2
θ_a	32 °C	Ambient temperature
θ_+	20.5 °C	Higher end of hysteresis band
θ_-	19.5 °C	Lower end of hysteresis band
θ	20 °C	Initial temperature set point for n ACs
σ_{rel}	0.2	defined as $\sigma_{rel}^2 = \sigma_C^2 / \mu_C^2$
σ_C^2	0.4	Variance of n ACs' heat capacity
σ_R^2	0.72	Variance of n ACs' thermal resistance
σ_P^2	1.2	Variance of n ACs' thermal power
H	1 °C	Hysteresis width of indoor temperature
COP (coefficient of performance)	2.5	Load efficiency

From Equations (12) - (19) it can be seen that, when the number of air conditioning in the load control activity is determined, the total power of the aggregated air conditioning group is related to the ambient temperature. Combined with the equivalent thermal parameters (ETP) model of ACs, we make the following simulation: When the outdoor temperatures were respectively [28, 28.5, 29, 29.5, 30, 31, 31.5, 32, 34, 34.5, 35, 35.5, 30.5, 36] ℃, assuming no control is applied, the baseline load power of the aggregated air conditioners is shown in Figure 2.

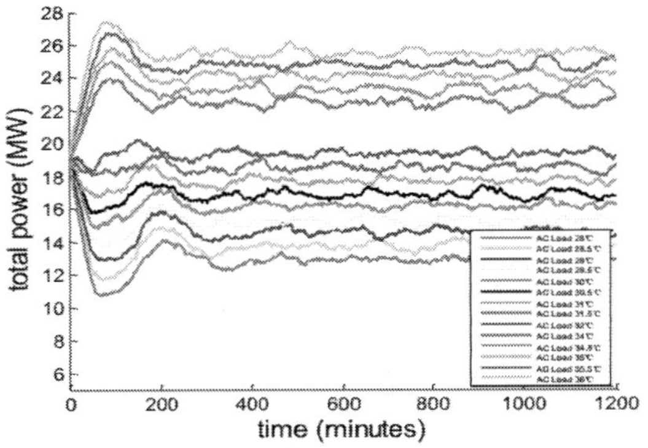

Figure 2. The power demand of the AC group at different outdoor temperatures

Figures 2 demonstrates that, without any control, the AC group will keep running independently. The profile of the aggregated demand of AC group is gentle, the duty cycle in steady state is 0.467. Because the initial duty is set to 0.446, the initial load of air-conditioning group is about 19 MW, the final load stabilized between 12 MW-26 MW. Such a conclusion can be drawn: The higher the outdoor temperature is, the higher the aggregate power of such population of ACs will be. On the contrary, the lower the outdoor temperature is, the lower the aggregate power of such population of ACs will be. When the ambient temperature is constant, assumed 32℃, the simulated parameters are listed in Table 2, whose parameters are subsequently calculated by using Equations (12)-(19).

Table 2. Parameters of second order linear time invariant transfer function.

Parameters	$D_{ss}(\theta)$	r	ξ	ω_n	$b_0 \times 10^{-4}$	b_1	b_2
Value	0.429	0.431	0.259	0.033	0.378	0.012	0.429

The whole load control scenario is from 12:00 p.m. to 16:00 p.m., during which the grid is in a peak load period. There is a power shortage and therefore needs a 20% reduction of air conditioning load. The load aggregator will raise the temperature set point of the ACs to achieve peak load shifting.

Figure 3 shows a comparison between the uncontrolled AC load, the desired reference value of the aggregated demand of a population of ACs for load shifting, and the actual output of ACs, when the outdoor temperature is constantly 32 ℃. The reason why the mismatch between the two figures exists only during the peak energy consumption lies in that, we only carry on the load control during peak hours and no control is performed outside this period. In Figure 3, the top blue curve is the 96 points AC load characteristic curve of the customers in the area on the maximum load day. We simulated the load values each second, by using the method of spline interpolation. Peak hours are from 12:00 a.m. to 16:00 p.m. During these periods, the electricity demand outstrips supply, and a power shortfall will appear. The top blue curve represents the aggregated power of 18,000 ACs without any control, the red dotted curve represents the desired AC load reference value for load shifting, and the solid black line represents the actual output power of AC load based on the proposed IMC controller and transfer function control model.

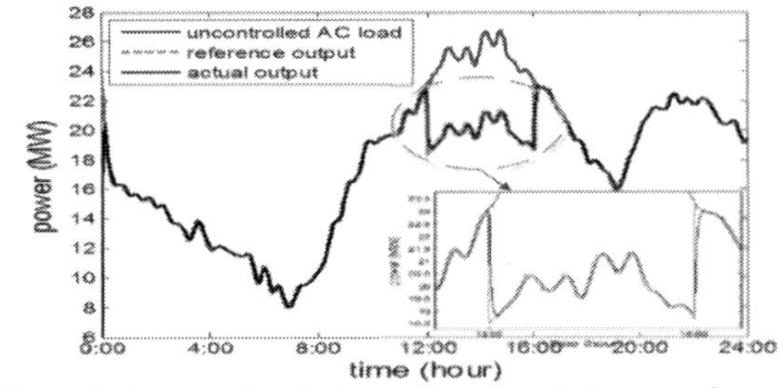

Figure 3. A comparison between the aggregated power of 18,000 ACs without any control, the desired AC load reference value for load shifting, and the actual output power of AC load based on the IMC controller, when the outdoor temperature is constantly 32 ℃

In this scenario, the second order transfer function of the AC group remains unchanged because of the constant ambient temperature. As can be seen from the figure, the effect of using the IMC controller is significantly good. Throughout the whole control period, the output power of the air conditionings has been following the reference value closely, and the tracking error is small. To some extent, the power shortage has been eased, and it meets with requires of rapidity, accuracy and stability of the control system.

5.2 Scenario 2: AC load control considering the influence of urban microclimate

In this scenario, the impact of urban microclimate on the air conditioning load control is considered. July 27th, 2015 is selected as a typical day, the period of load control is still selected from 12:00 p.m. to 16:00 p.m., like the scenario 1. For during this period, Nanjing experiences the hottest weather and the maximum air conditioning load.

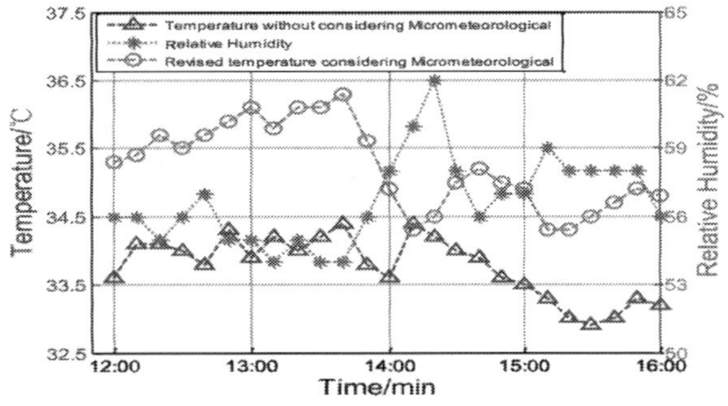

Figure 4. A comparison between the temperature before being modified (blue line) without considering urban microclimate, relative humidity (green line), and the modified temperature (red line) according to the influence of urban microclimate.

The heat island intensity is obtained by using the temperature inversion algorithm of the heat island effect. Then, the heat index is calculated by combining temperature and humidity. Based on the above microclimate, the ambient temperature index of urban central area is modified. Figure 4 shows a comparison between the temperature before being modified (blue line) without considering urban microclimate, relative humidity (green line), and the modified temperature (red line) according to the influence of urban microclimate. The real-time temperature and relative humidity on the same day, which was collected every 10 min, was provided by the Jiangsu Provincial Meteorological Bureau.

In this scenario, we consider a more realistic situation, which means an ever-changing ambient temperature. It is dynamically modified in real time and constantly changing, depending on the weather conditions and urban microclimatic. Based on the expression of the second order transfer function model of the aggregate ACs (12)-(19), if the outdoor temperature varies with time, the second order transfer function model of the aggregated AC group will no longer be linear time invariant. Instead, it is changing with time. The model parameters vary with the outdoor temperature in the case of equivalent thermal resistance, thermal capacitance and other parameters remaining unchanged. Changes in the parameters of the second order transfer function of ACs are shown in Figure 5. The actual value of the ambient temperature was measured at weather stations on 15 August July 27th, 2015, and the period is from 12:00 p.m. to 16:00 p.m..

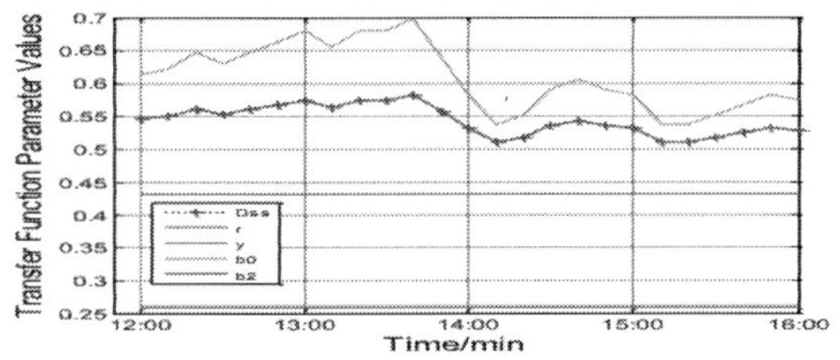

(a)

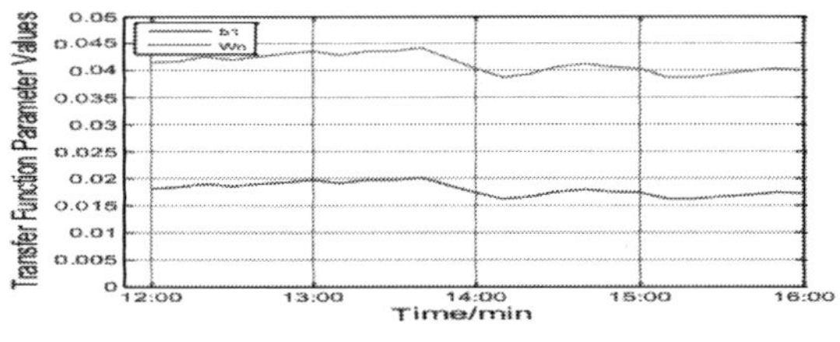

(b)

Figure 5. Changes in the parameters of the second order linear time varying transfer function model of ACs

In the simulation, the linear time invariant model of the aggregated ACs in Scenario 1 is changed into a time varying model. In Simulink simulation, if the parameters of the transfer function are changed, the response of the transfer function to the time domain is also changed. Subsequently, the effective length of the calculation may change, and this will result in a difficulty for simulink to calculate the transfer function with the ever-changing parameters.

The whole load control scenario is still from 12:00 p.m. to 16:00 p.m. Figure 6 illustrates the impact of urban microclimate on air-conditioning load control in the urban central area. The profiles are obtained by simulating the two order linear time invariant transfer function model, which is based on the parameters in Table 1 and the modified ambient temperature curve in Figure 4. The upper blue curve represents the aggregated baseline power of 18,000 ACs without any control, the middle red dashed curve is the desired AC load reference value for load shifting, the solid green curve is AC load curve obtained by the second order transfer function model for n ACs and the modified ambient temperature heat index based on urban microclimate, and the dashed black line at the bottom represents the AC load control effect without considering urban microclimate. A comparison of probability density distribution of the tracking error between the load control without considering urban microclimate and the load control considering urban microclimate is shown in Figure 7. As can be seen, without considering urban microclimate, the probability density is maximal when the load tracking error is 0. In the case of considering urban micro climate in a more realistic scenario, the probability density is maximal when the load tracking error is 1.5MW.

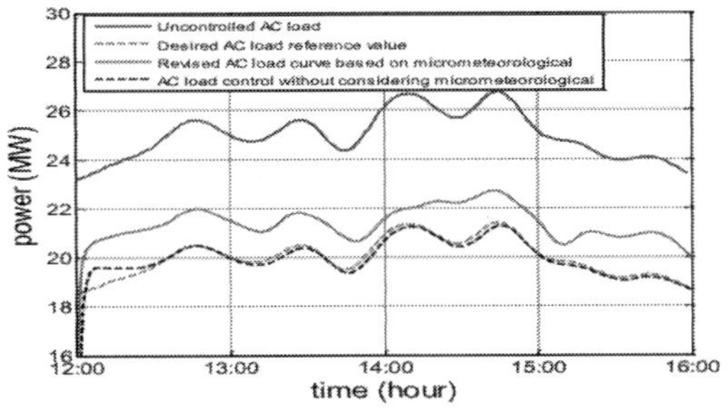

Figure 6. The impact of urban microclimate on air-conditioning load control in the urban central area.

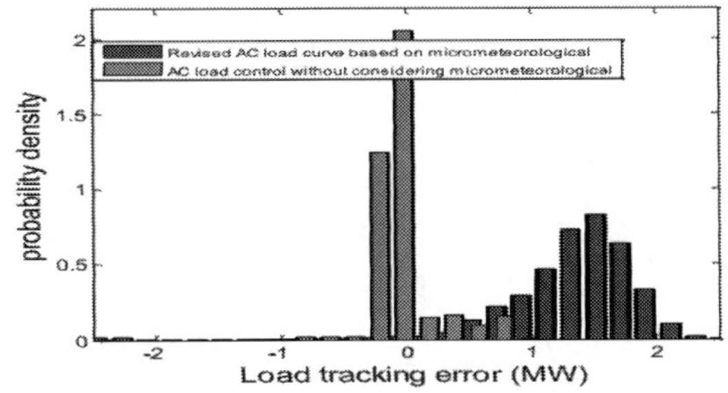

Figure 7. A comparison of probability density distribution of the tracking error between the load control without considering urban microclimate and the load control considering urban microclimate.

The performance of load control in the simulation is very good when the impact of the urban microclimate is not taken into account. Under the influence of urban microclimate, the maximum load of ACs participated in direct load control (DLC) is changed from 22.8MW to 21.2MW. But it is still far less than 26.8MW when there is no load control. As can be seen from the simulation results, because of the existence of urban microclimate, the potential of load control is reduced to 71.43% of the original.

6 Conclusions

The design of a closed-loop control strategy for AC loads to participate in load control was presented, and an IMC controller was also developed in this paper. Parameters of the model will be influenced by the ambient temperature and urban microclimate. The main contribution of this paper can be summarised as following: The heat island intensity is obtained by using the temperature inversion algorithm of the heat island effect. Then, the heat index is calculated by combining temperature and humidity. Based on the above urban microclimate, the ambient temperature index of urban central area is modified, and the second order linear time invariant model of aggregated ACs is upgraded to the linear time varying model. The consequent parameter changes of the second order transfer function model are studied and the influence of urban microclimate on AC load control is analyzed.

In fact, because of the inevitable existence of urban micro climate (e.g. heat island effect, the temperature and humidity effect), the apparent temperature is higher than the actual environmental temperature, resulting in an impact on the comfort of the occupants. Then the residents need to reduce the temperature set point of ACs to stay comfortable. As a result, the actual air-conditioning energy consumption rises, and the load control effect of ACs will be worse to some extent. From the simulation results it can also be seen that, the tendency of the AC load profile based on the proposed control model and control strategy is consistent with the desired AC load reference value.

References

1. C. Li, J. Zhou, Y. Cao, et al. Interaction between urban microclimate and electric air-conditioning energy consumption during high temperature season. Applied Energy, 117: 149-156 (2014).
2. C. Li, J. Shang, S. Zhu, et al. An analysis of energy consumption caused by air temperature affected accumulative effect of the air conditioning load. Automat Electric Power Syst, 34(20):30-32, (2010).
3. L. Yao, H. R. Lu. A second-way direct control of central air-conditioning load via the internet. IEEE Trans. on Power Delivery, vol. 24, no.1, 240-248 (2009).
4. T. Ojima, Changing Tokyo metropolitan area and its heat island model. Energy and Buildings, 15(1): 191-203,(1991).
5. M. Santamouris, N. Papanikolaou, I. Livada, et al. On the impact of urban climate on the energy consumption of buildings. Solar energy, 70(3): 201-216, (2001).
6. S. Hassid, M. Santamouris, N. Papanikolaou, et al. The effect of the Athens heat island on air conditioning load. Energy and Buildings, 32(2): 131-141(2000).

7. X. T. Li. Effects of urbanization on cooling load of residential buildings. Heating Ventilating and Air Conditioning, 32(2): 79-81, (2002).
8. D. S. Callaway, I. A. Hiskens, Achieving Controllability of Electric Loads, Proceedings of the IEEE, 1, 184-199,(2011).
9. S. Kundu, N. Sinitsyn, S. Backhaus, and I. Hiskens, Modeling and Control of Thermostatically Controlled Loads. Available online: http://arxiv.org/abs/1101.2157 (accessed on 10 August 2015).
10. X. Hu,; B. Wang, S. Yang, T. Short, and L. A. Zhou, Closed-Loop Control Strategy for Air Conditioning Loads to Participate in Demand Response. Energies, 8, 8650-8681(2015).
11. J. C. Jiménez-Muñoz, and J. A.Sobrino, A generalized single - channel method for retrieving land surface temperature from remote sensing data. Journal of Geophysical Research: Atmospheres (1984–2012), 108(D22),(2012).
12. L. P. Rothfusz, The heat index 'equation' (or, more than you ever wanted to know about heat index). NWS Technical Attachment SR90-23. NWS Southern Region Headquarters, Fort Worth, TX.

MATEC Web of Conferences **50**, 01004 (2016)
DOI: 10.1051/matecconf/20165001004

Experimental Investigation of the Corona Discharge in Electrical Transmission due to AC/DC Electric Fields

Phanupong Fuangpian, Taimoor Zafar, Sayan Ruankorn and Thanapong Suwanasri

The Sirindhorn International Thai-German Graduate School of Engineering, King Mongkut's University of Technology North Bangkok, Bangkok, Thailand

Abstract. Nowadays, using of High Voltage Direct Current (HVDC) transmission to maximize the transmission efficiency, bulk power transmission, connection of renewable power source from wind farm to the grid is of prime concern for the utility. However, due to the high electric field stress from Direct Current (DC) line, the corona discharge can easily be occurred at the conductor surface leading to transmission loss. Therefore, the polarity effect of DC lines on corona inception and breakdown voltage should be investigated. In this work, the effect of DC polarity and Alternating Current (AC) field stress on corona inception voltage and corona discharge is investigated on various test objects, such as High Voltage (HV) needle, needle at ground plane, internal defect, surface discharge, underground cable without cable termination, cable termination with simulated defect and bare overhead conductor. The corona discharge is measured by partial discharge measurement device with high-frequency current transformer. Finally, the relationship between supply voltage and discharge intensity on each DC polarity and AC field stress can be successfully determined.

1 Introduction

High Voltage Direct Current has been used in electrical transmission for several decades for bulk electric power transmission, interconnection of systems with different frequencies, undersea cable transmission and connection of off-shore wind farm to electrical grid. Using of HVDC creates high electric field stress on the conductor surface and its surroundings. For this reason, it is easier than alternating current voltage in electrical transmission system for corona inception and corona discharge as well as interference to communication system nearby [1]. The most effective DC transmission is bipolar with one positive and one negative conductor on the same tower. Thus, the effect of polarity on corona inception and corona discharge must be investigated and compared with that of AC electric field stress [2]. The onset of corona and subsequent growing discharge can be detected by using partial discharge measurement system with an appropriate sensor for effective detection. The experimental test setup consists of HVDC generation by half-wave rectifier with smoothing capacitor [3], partial discharge measurement system using high-frequency current transformer (HFCT) as a non-conventional detection method [4], [5] and various test objects. The first group of test object is HV needle, needle at ground, surface and internal discharge inside solid insulation as basic test object for theoretical comparison. The second group of test object is underground cable, which is examined without cable termination for surface discharge generation and underground cable with simulated defect. The third group of test object is bare overhead conductor in the small scale model to observe the effect of AC/DC electric field stress. The experiments are performed with every test object by supplying DC voltage of both polarities as well as AC voltage to find the corona inception voltage and the relationship between corona discharge amplitude and the magnitude of the supply voltage.

2 Experimental Setup

2.1 Corona discharge and its detection

Corona discharge is theoretically a localized partial discharge, which can not bridge the gap between electrodes. The corona discharge can occur in transmission system because the high electric field stress at the sharp edge ionizes the air molecules surrounding it. This creates loss in transmission system, which should be prevented in the fair weather condition. Corona discharge can be detected by using non-conventional partial discharge sensor such as Ultra High Frequency (UHF) antenna, acoustic sensor or HFCT. Among various sensor types, HFCT provides an accurate result because it measures the electrical discharge pulse flowing to ground through ground conductor. During testing, the supplied AC and DC voltages are gradually increased until corona or partial discharge is detected by HFCT sensor.

2.2 Test Circuit

The test circuit is shown in Figure 1.

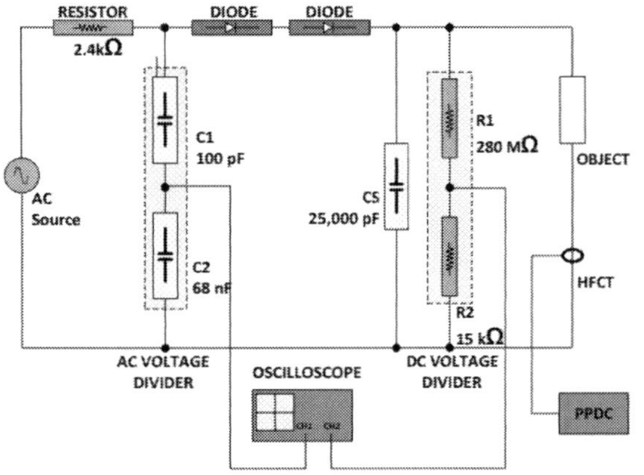

Figure 1. Test circuit for DC voltage generation and partial discharge measurements

The test circuit consists of:

1. High voltage DC generation by using half-wave rectifier: 100 kV insulated tank type test transformer, 2 diodes and 25,000 pF smoothing capacitor (C_S).
2. The generated high voltage DC is measured by resistive voltage divider: R1 = 280 MΩ and R2 = 15 kΩ resistors.
3. The corona inception voltage, corona discharge as well as partial discharge in another form are measured by using portable PD check device from TECHIMP with a high-frequency current transformer as a non-conventional sensor to detect PD pulse to ground at ground conductor.

The tests are performed in a partly shielded high voltage laboratory with background noise less than 5 pC or 2 mV by HFCT.

2.2 Test Objects

The test objects are divided into 3 groups as follows:

1. Basic test object for theoretical comparison e.g. HV needle, needle at ground, surface and internal discharge inside solid insulation. The needle at HV and internal discharge test objects are presented in Figure 2. To avoid the surface discharge during internal discharge test, the test object is immersed in the transformer insulating oil as shown in Figure 2 (b).
2. Underground cable, which is used without cable termination for surface discharge generation and underground cable with simulated defect by particle and impurity. Figure 3 shows the underground cable without termination and defected termination under test.
3. Bare overhead conductor in the small scale model. The bare copper wire is installed on the solid supporting insulator.

(a) (b)

Figure 2. Basic test objects as needle at HV (a) and internal discharge (b)

(a) (b)

Figure 3. Underground cable under test, without termination (a) and defected termination (b)

The tests are performed by gradually increasing the supplied voltage to the test object until the corona discharges are initiated. This minimum voltage causing the corona discharges is recorded as corona inception voltage. Then, the supplied voltage is gradually increased further and the corona discharge amplitude is recorded until the breakdown is occurred. After that, the same test is performed again on the object with reversed polarity of DC voltage and AC voltage subsequently.

3 Experimental Results

The corona inception voltage and the relationship between supplied voltage and corona/partial discharge amplitude for each test object are presented in this section.

3.1. Basic Test Object

The corona inception voltage in case of positive and negative polarity is listed in Table 1 and the relationship between corona/partial discharge amplitude and supplied voltage is presented in Figure 4.

The first object is needle at high voltage terminal. The measured inception voltage for negative polarity is lower than that of positive polarity. However, the corona discharge amplitude at the instant of inception for negative polarity is 13 mV, which is lower than that of positive polarity 47 mV. This result agrees well with the theory as the corona inception voltage of negative DC is lower than positive due to positive space charge close to the rod tip creating higher electric field stress at negative rod. The discharge amplitude of positive DC is greater than negative due to space charge accumulation.

The second object is needle at ground plane and plate at high voltage terminal. The measured inception voltage value of both the polarities is equal. However, the corona discharge amplitude at the instant of inception for negative polarity is 68 mV, which is greater than that of positive polarity 12 mV. The result of corona discharge amplitude is now reversed because when the high voltage at plate is positive and the needle is grounded, it is similar to negative voltage at needle. Similarly, when the high voltage at plate is negative and the needle is grounded, it is similar to positive voltage at needle.

The third object is internal defect with air void inside solid insulation. The measured inception voltage of negative polarity is lower than that of positive polarity. However, the corona discharge amplitude at the instant of inception for negative polarity is 14 mV, which is lower than that of positive polarity 34 mV. It can also be clearly seen that the corona discharge amplitude of positive polarity after inception increases significantly, whereas that of negative polarity remains at lower amplitude.

The fourth object is surface discharge along solid insulation. The measured inception voltage in case of negative polarity is lower than that of positive polarity. However, the corona discharge amplitude at the instant of inception for negative polarity is 21 mV, which is lower than that of positive polarity 703 mV. The corona discharge amplitude of positive polarity after inception increases significantly, whereas that of negative polarity remains at lower amplitude.

Table 1. Corona inception voltage of basic test object due to polarity effect

Test Object	Corona Inception Voltage (Positive)	Corona Inception Voltage (Negative)
Needle at HV	5 kV	4 kV
Needle at Ground	6 kV	6 kV
Internal Defect	35 kV	22 kV
Surface Discharge	14 kV	11 kV

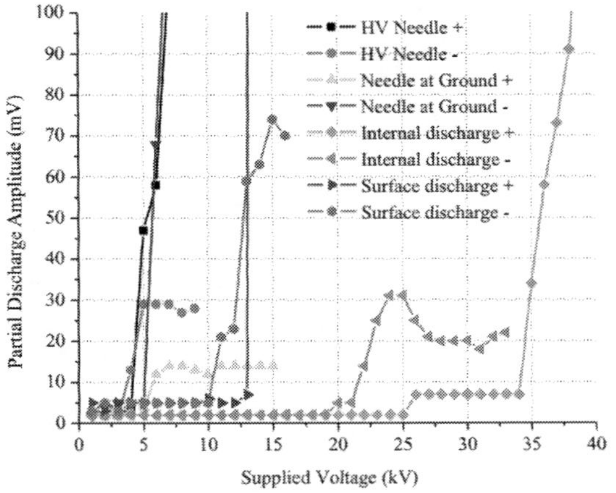

Figure 4. Relationship between corona discharge amplitude and supplied voltage of basic test object

From the partial discharge measurement results of needle at high voltage during corona inception shown in Figure 5, the corona discharge of positive polarity has greater amplitude with large dispersion of amplitude than that of negative polarity due to space charge effect. However, the frequency of occurrence from discharge waveform in time domain is less than negative polarity. The corona discharge of negative polarity has smaller amplitude but occurs more frequently. Figure 6 shows the corona discharge waveform of internal discharge inside solid insulation. The discharge amplitude of positive polarity is relatively greater than negative polarity, but the discharge waveforms in time domain of both polarities are nearly similar.

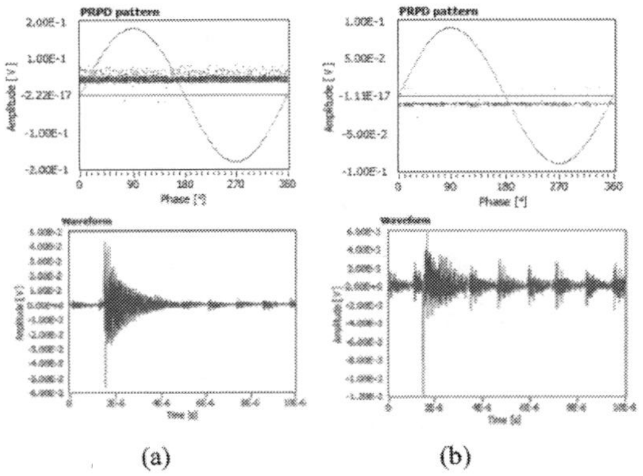

Figure 5. Partial discharge pattern of needle at high voltage for positive (a) and negative (b) polarity

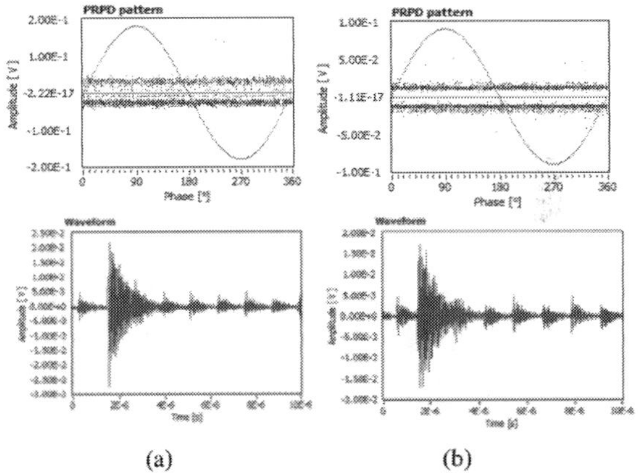

Figure 6. Partial discharge pattern of internal discharge inside solid insulation for positive (a) and negative (b) polarity

3.2 Underground Cable

The underground cable rated voltage 3.6/6 (7.2) kV with XLPE insulation are used in this test. The corona inception voltage and the relationship between corona/partial discharge amplitude and supplied voltage are listed in Table 2 and presented in Figure 7, respectively.

The first object is underground cable without cable termination for surface discharge generation along the XLPE insulation surface due to high electric field stress at the outer semiconductor shield. The measured inception voltage for both polarities is equal, but it is greater than that of AC voltage. However, the surface discharge amplitude at the instant of inception is different, which is 100 mV, 15 mV and 38 mV for positive polarity, negative polarity and AC voltage respectively. Then, this cable without termination can withstand surface discharge from DC less than that of AC voltage due to continuous electric field stress.

The second object is underground cable with defected cable termination. The surface between XLPE insulation and termination was contaminated by particle and impurity. The measured inception voltage of positive polarity is slightly greater than that of negative polarity. However, the corona inception voltage in case of AC voltage is slightly greater than DC voltage. The partial discharge amplitude at the instant of inception is significantly different, which is 441 mV, 27 mV and 13 mV for positive polarity, negative polarity and AC voltage respectively.

Table 2. Corona inception voltage of underground cable and defected cable termination due to polarity effect

Test Object	Corona Inception Voltage (Positive)	Corona Inception Voltage (Negative)	Corona Inception Voltage (AC)
Cable without termination	12 kV	12 kV	6 kV
Termination with impurity	16 kV	15 kV	17 kV

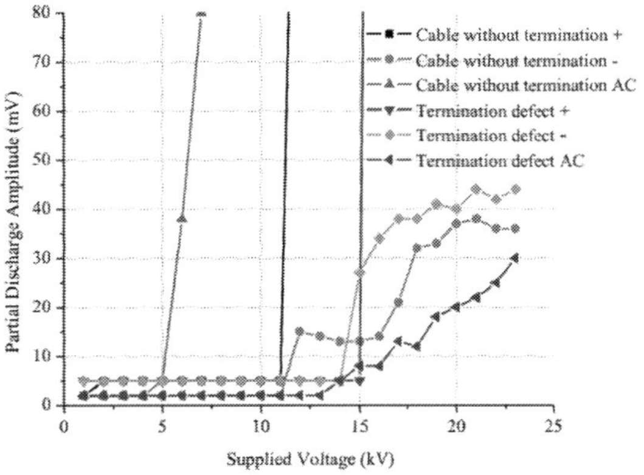

Figure 7. Relationship between supplied voltage and corona discharge amplitude for cable without termination and with defected cable termination

It can be clearly seen that the partial discharge pattern of DC electric field stress is constant with small dispersion of discharge amplitude due to space charge effect. This discharge pattern is different from AC field because of the constant electric field from DC supply. The partial discharge pattern of underground cable without termination for AC voltage in Figure 8 shows the surface discharge pattern [2] due to high electric field stress at the outer semiconducting shield.

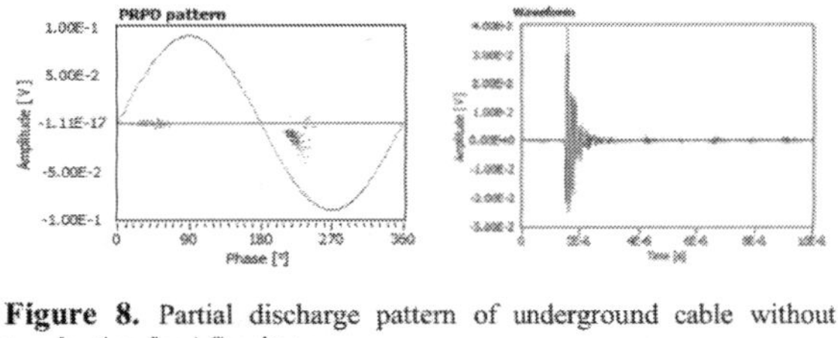

Figure 8. Partial discharge pattern of underground cable without termination for AC voltage

The effect of DC voltage polarity on discharge amplitude and waveform can be seen in Figure 9. The discharge waveform of positive polarity has greater amplitude with single discharge pulse, whereas that of negative polarity has less amplitude with higher frequency of occurrence or higher repetition rate.

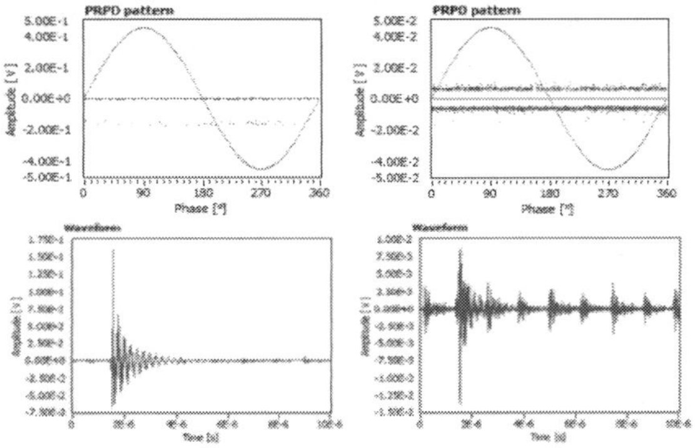

(a) (b)

Figure 9. Partial discharge pattern of underground cable without termination for positive (a) and negative (b) polarity

3.3 Bare Conductor

The corona inception voltage and the relationship between corona/partial discharge amplitude and supplied voltage is listed in Table 3 and presented in Figure 10.

The measured inception voltage of positive polarity is greater than that of negative polarity and AC voltage. Moreover, the corona discharge amplitude at the instant of inception for positive polarity (137 mV) is significantly greater than that of negative polarity (11 mV) and AC voltage (11 mV). The corona discharge amplitude of positive polarity after inception increases significantly, whereas that of negative polarity and AC voltage remains at lower amplitude.

Table 3. Corona inception voltage of bare conductor due to polarity effect

Test Object	Corona Inception Voltage (Positive)	Corona Inception Voltage (Negative)	Corona Inception Voltage (AC)
Bare Conductor	15 kV	12 kV	12 kV

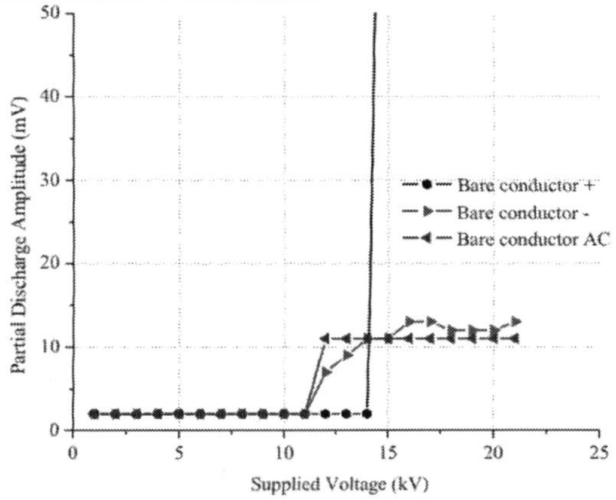

Figure 10. Relationship between supplied voltage and corona discharge amplitude of bare conductor

The partial discharge pattern of bare conductor for AC voltage shown in Figure 11 is the corona discharge at the negative cycle of sinusoidal waveform because the energized bare conductor is at high voltage potential. The effect of DC voltage polarity on discharge amplitude and waveform can be seen in Figure 12. The discharge waveform of positive polarity has greater amplitude with single discharge pulse, whereas that of negative polarity has smaller amplitude with higher frequency of occurrence. This result agrees well with the corona discharge observed from HV needle in basic test object.

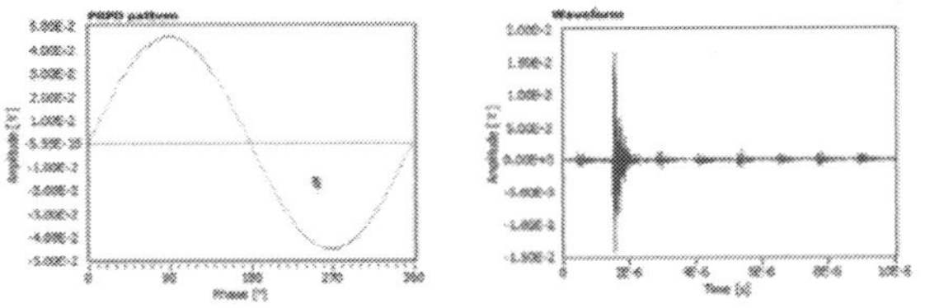

Figure 11. Partial discharge pattern of bare conductor for AC voltage

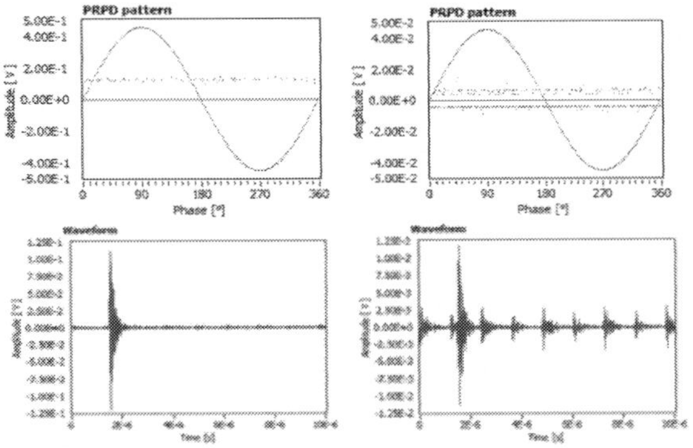

(a) (b)

Figure 12. Partial discharge pattern of bare conductor for positive (a) and negative (b) polarity

4 Conclusions

The effect of DC polarity and AC field stress on corona inception voltage as well as partial discharge amplitude and pattern has been investigated on various test objects, such as HV needle, needle at ground plane, internal defect, surface discharge, underground cable without cable termination, cable termination with simulated defect and bare overhead conductor. The corona discharge and partial discharge from test objects are measured by using HFCT to detect the discharge pulse flowing to ground. The measured discharge waveform of positive polarity has greater amplitude with single discharge pulse, whereas that of negative polarity has less amplitude with higher frequency of occurrence or higher repetition rate. Then, the inception voltage of positive DC is usually greater than those of negative polarity and AC voltage. Because of the lower corona and partial discharge inception voltage of negative DC, the corona and partial discharge of negative DC occur more frequent than positive DC as higher repetition rate, however with less severity. The result can be further used to design the proper insulation and size of conductor for HVDC applications.

References

1. A. G. Swanson and I. R. Jandrell, *Investigation into HVDC corona: discussion and initial modelling results*, The XVII International Symposium on High Voltage Engineering, Hannover, Germany, August 22-26 (2011)
2. CIGRE Working Group 21.03, Recognition of Discharges, Electra, No. **11**, pp. 61-98 (1969)
3. J. Kuffel, E. Kuffel, W. S. Zaengl, *High voltage engineering fundamentals*, Butterworth-Heinemann/ Newnes, Oxford, Boston (2000)
4. C. Suwanasri, T. Suwanasri and P. Fuangpian, *Investigation on Partial Discharge of Power Cable Termination Defects using High Frequency Current Transformer*, ECTI Transactions on Electrical Eng., Electronics and Communications Vol. **12**, No. **1**, page 16 – 23 (2014)
5. S. Birlasekaran, and Weng Hoe Leong, *Comparison of Known PD Signals with the Developed and Commercial HFCT Sensors*, IEEE Trans. Power Delivery, Vol. **22**, Issue. **3**, pp. 1581-1590 (2007)

MATEC Web of Conferences **50**, 02001 (2016)
DOI: 10.1051/matecconf/20165002001

DC-link Voltage Control to Compensate Voltage Deviation for PV–BESSs Integrated System in Low-Voltage (LV) Networks

Gyu-sub Lee, Yun-su Kim , Jae-won Chang and Seung-il Moon

Seoul National University (SNU), Electrical Engineering Department, 08826 Gwanak-gu Seoul, Republic of Korea

Abstract. The exhaustion of fossil fuel and the greenhouse gas emission are one of the most significant energy and environmental issues, respectively. Photovoltaic (PV) generators and battery energy storage systems (BESSs) have been significantly increased for recent years. The BESSs are mainly used for smoothing active power fluctuation of the PV. In this paper, PV–BESSs integration of two DC/DC converters and one AC/DC converter is investigated and DC-link voltage control to compensate the AC voltage deviation is proposed for the PV–BESS system in low-voltage (LV) networks.

1 Introduction

The exhaustion of fossil fuel and environmental pollution have made high interest toward renewable energies. Therefore, researches on grid-connected photovoltaic (PV) systems have been significantly increased. The PV systems can be adopted in both low-voltage (LV) systems and higher voltage system. Numorous researches on the PV systems have been studied, especially on integrating PV–energy storage system (ESS) have been increased in recent years. Since the active power fluctuation of the PV system may make the system unstable, the ESSs are mainly used with the PV systems to prevent the system from instability. For instance, providing an average power reference to the PV system may help the stable operation of the PV–ESS integrated system in the perspective of smoothing active power.

Two types of the PV–ESS integrated systems shown in Figure 1 are investigated in this paper. An AC integrating system, depicted in Figure 1(a), uses two AC/DC converters on smoothing PV fluctuation. On the other hand, a DC integrating system, depicted in Figure 1(b), uses one AC/DC converter. In the DC integrating system, two DC/DC converters should be installed for voltage stability of a common DC bus. Control strategies of the DC/DC converters and operation scheme of PV–ESS systems were proposed in [1-6]. High-gain DC/DC converters and control strategies for large-scale PV systems were proposed in [1]. Basic operation scheme of the PV-ESS system with DC integration was investigated in [2]. However, existing method didn't consider an abnormal condition of BESS and only used the BESS output for smoothing.

Unlike general high or medium voltage system, X/R ratios of LV systems are under 0.5. Because a resistive component is much bigger than an inductive component, voltage fluctuation is highly dependent on active power fluctuation. Therefore the high penetration of intermittent renewable energy sources (RESs) in the LV networks may cause voltage instability. Various types of voltage control methods in the LV networks were investigated and proposed in [7-10]. The voltage–active power (V–P) droop control method was proposed and basic formulations of active and reactive power in the LV network were investigated in [7]. Relationships between voltage and active power proposed in above papers are used for proposed method. Characteristics of the LV systems are investigated in [8-9].

By smoothing active power fluctuation of PV using ESS, battery state-of-charge (SOC) should be undesirably deviated from the scheduled value. However the deviation may make the SOC value exceed the limit. An excess of the SOC limit causes under-voltage or over-voltage in the steady-state. other papers didn't consider how SOC limit affects to stability of systems. In this paper, the system voltage compensation method is proposed to mitigate voltage deviation. The proposed method was applied to the PV–ESS integrated system and tested by MATLAB/SimPowerSystems to prove its effectiveness.

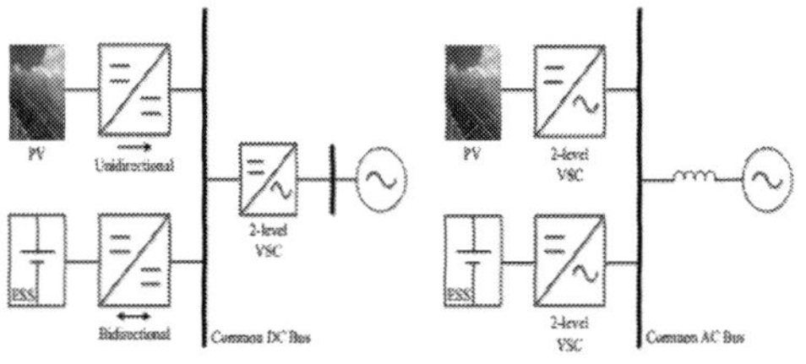

(a) (b)

Figure 1. Two types of PV–ESS integration method

2 Modeling

2.1 Battery Energy Storage System (BESS)

The BESSs are composed of DC voltage ans state-of-charge (SOC). A simple battery model has proportional DC voltage to SOC. DC voltage deviation from the SOC is not considered in this paper. SOC is simply regarded as energy remaining of battery. SOC at time $t_0+\Delta t$ is modeled as equation (1).

$$SOC_{t_0+\Delta t} = SOC_{t_0} - \int_{t_0}^{t_0+\Delta t} \frac{I_{dc}}{Q_c} dt \qquad (1)$$

where, Q_c is capacity of the battery

2.2 DC/DC Converter

There are two types of DC/DC converters in DC integrated systems. One is the DC/DC converter used in connecting the PV and a common DC bus. The other is the converter used in connecting the BESSs and the common DC bus. Current of the DC/DC converter used in the PV integrating is always positive so buck-boost converter topology is used. On the other hand, bi-directional buck-boost converter topology is used in integrating the BESSs and the common DC bus. Figure 2 is the one-way buck-boost topology and Figure 3 is the bi-directional buck-boost converter topology which are used in the PV-ESS integrated systems.

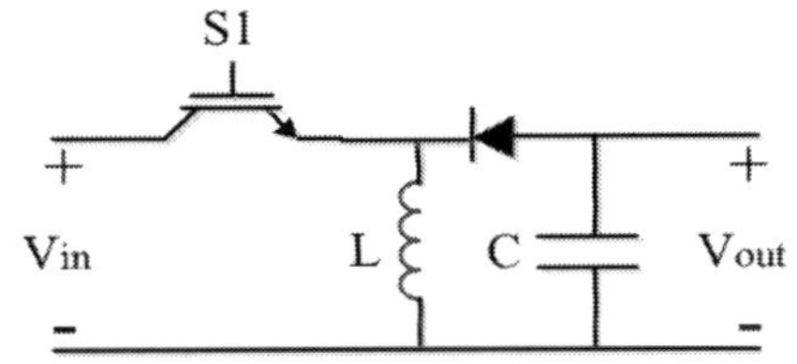

Figure 2. Simple buck-boost converter topology

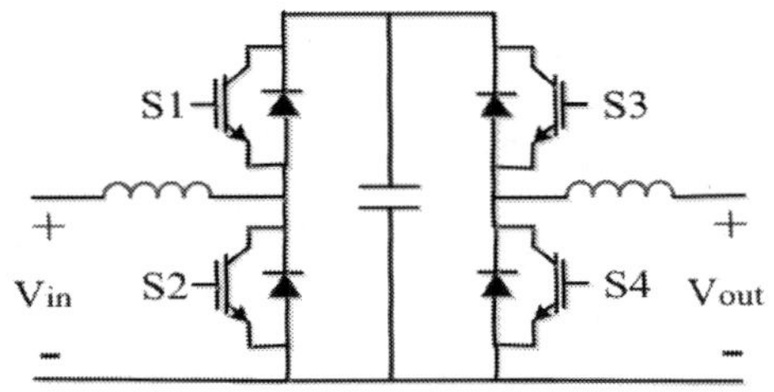

Figure 3. Bi-directional buck-boost converter topology

Both two converters have gains from 0 to inf. ideally. The DC/DC converter connected to the PV operates at maximum power point tracking (MPPT) control scheme. For using actual measurement data of the PV power, assuming the MPPT control is successfully conducted is valid. So the PV-connected DC/DC converter is operated by power referenced control scheme. The control scheme of the buck-boost converter is shown in Figure 4.

In the PV–BESSs integrated systems, output power of BESSs is a difference between the PV average power and the actual power. The PV average power can be calculated in many ways. The BESSs-connected DC/DC converter is also operated by power referenced control scheme and the power reference is calculated from the actual PV output power and the average output power. The control scheme of bi-directional converter is shown in Figure 5.

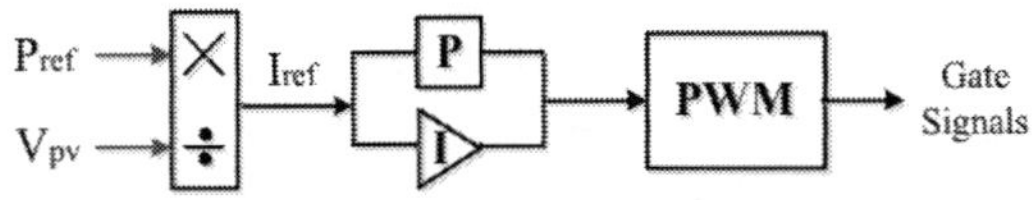

Figure 4. The control scheme of simple buck-boost converter

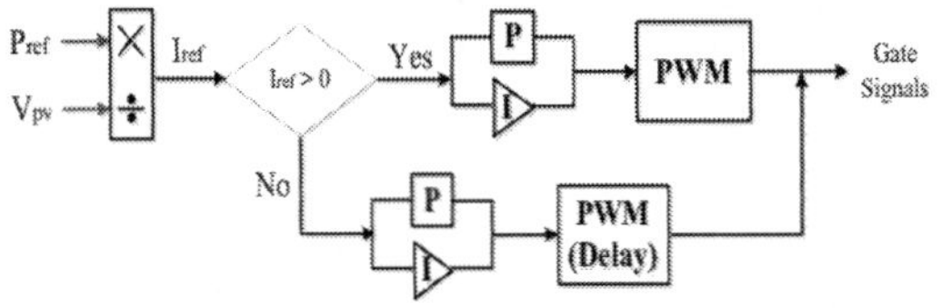

Figure 5. The control scheme of bi-directional converter

2.3 AC/DC Converter

Half-bridge 2-level voltage sourced converter (VSC) is used in the PV–ESS integrated systems. DC voltage of the common DC bus should be maintained constant. Therefore V_{dc}-Q control scheme is used in the AC/DC converter. The control scheme is shown in Figure 6.

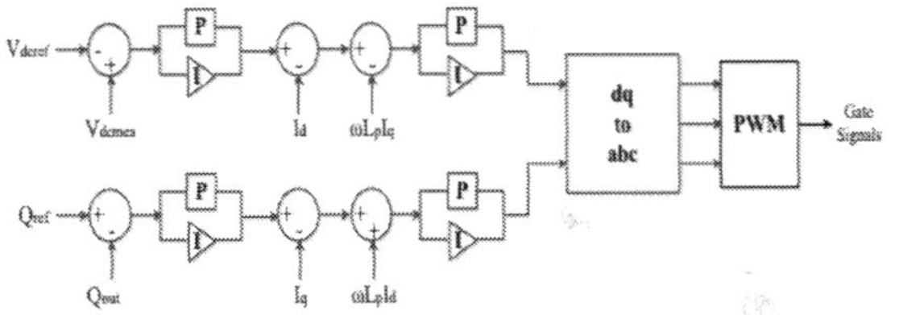

Figure 6. The control scheme of AC/DC converter

3 DC Voltage Compensation Method

3.1 Formulation

We can define a duty ratio (D) of the AC/DC converter which means time ratio positive voltage is applied at AC systems. Using the duty ratio, relation between V_{dc} and magnitude of equivalent AC voltage ($|V_{ac}|$) is shown in equation (2).

$$|V_{ac}|_{eq} = D(V_{dc}/2) + (1-D)(-V_{dc}/2) = (D - 1/2)V_{dc} \quad (2)$$

Equation (2) implies that steady-state AC voltage magnitude is proportional to DC voltage and the duty ratio. By using a Pulse Width Modulation (PWM), D should be changed continuously. On the other hand, DC voltage reference can be changed instantaneously.

3.2 SOC Limit

General the BESSs control scheme contains ON/OFF selector based on the SOC level. If the BESSs are on charging state, the SOC is increasing proportional to DC current. Otherwise, the SOC is decreasing. At $SOC_{min} < SOC < SOC_{max}$, the BESSs can operate in both charging and discharging state. If the $SOC=SOC_{min}$, BESSs cannot operate in discharging state. And BESSs cannot operate in charging state at the $SOC=SOC_{max}$.

This ON/OFF selector can make sudden output power decrease or increase because the SOC limit changes the BESSs operate mode instantaneously. This discontinuity makes output decrease or increase in steady-state. If the connected AC grid is the low-voltage (LV) system, sudden output deviation may cause voltage instability. DC-link voltage control scheme to compensate voltage deviation is proposed to relax the voltage instability

3.3 DC-link Voltage Control for Compensation

Sudden BESS off-signal due to SOC minimum value make voltage drop of AC bus. If the BESS control block operates on discharging state for a long time, under-voltage condition lasts for a long time. Sudden increase of DC voltage reference value can relax the under-voltage condition because $|V_{ac}|$ is proportional to V_{dc}. Over-voltage condition is also be relaxed by V_{dc} compensation.

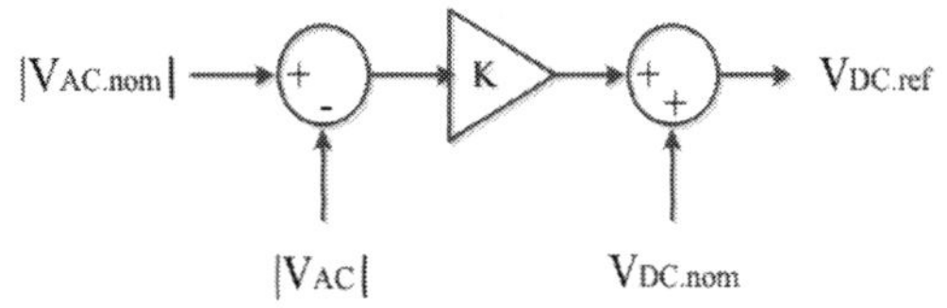

Figure 7. DC-link voltage control block

DC-link voltage control block to compensate voltage deviation is shown in Figure 7. Because compensation method can cause bad effect to smoothing the PV output, compensation gain should be adjusted to appropriate value [7]. This control scheme can be applied at low-voltage system. In the next section, we validate proposed method using simulation

4 Simulation

This section presents simulation results of the PV-BESS DC integrated module and proposed method. MATLAB/SimPowerSystems simulation tools are used in validation. Table 1 is the parameters used for the proposed PV system.

Table 1. The parameter used for simulation

PV Module	
DC Voltage (Vdc)	150 V
Maximum Output	50 kW
BESS Module	
DC Voltage (Vdc)	600 V
Maximum Ouput	50 kW
Capacity (Q)	160 A·sec
DC/DC Converter (Bi-directional)	
Switching Frequency	18000 Hz
Input Inductor	10 mH
Output Inductor	1 mH
Capacitor	500 μF
Other Parameter	
DC Bus Voltage	800 V
Grid Voltage (Line-to-Line)	560 V
Grid Frequency	60 Hz
X/R Ratio	0.15

For validation of SOC minimum limit, we assume that output of BESS is always positive in the simulation. Also sum of DC current references of PV and BESS is constant. In the simulation, the value is 2.5 (pu). PV data is actual measurement data of Hokkaido, Japan. We use the data with time scaling because actual fluctuation is less severe than expected one. SOC minimum limit is 0.2. Figure 8 is simulation results of under-voltage situation without DC voltage compensation. Figure 9 is simulation results of under-voltage situation with DC voltage compensation. Table 2 shows steady-state AC voltage before and after BESS is off.

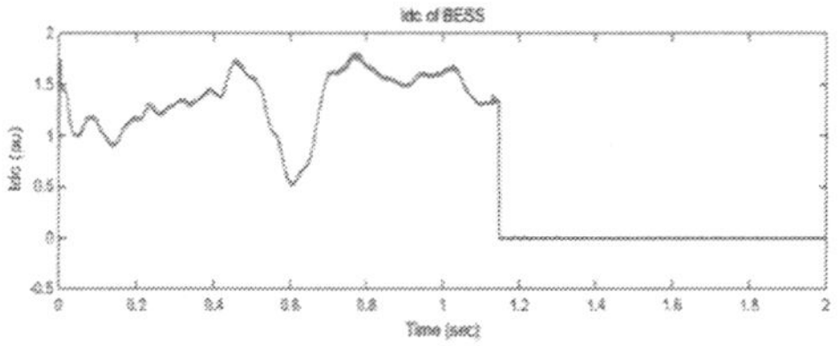

(a) DC current of BESS

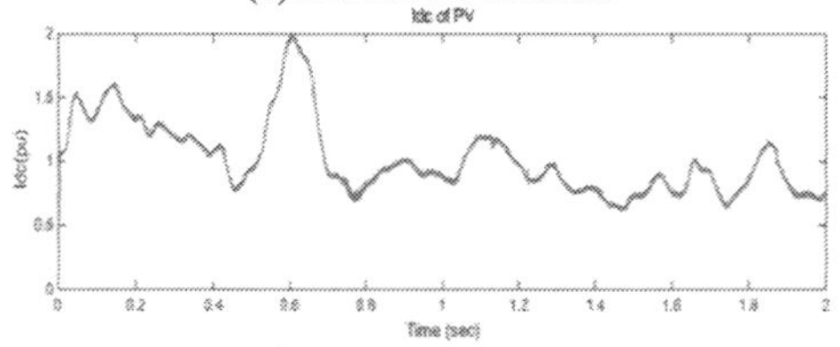

(b) DC current of PV

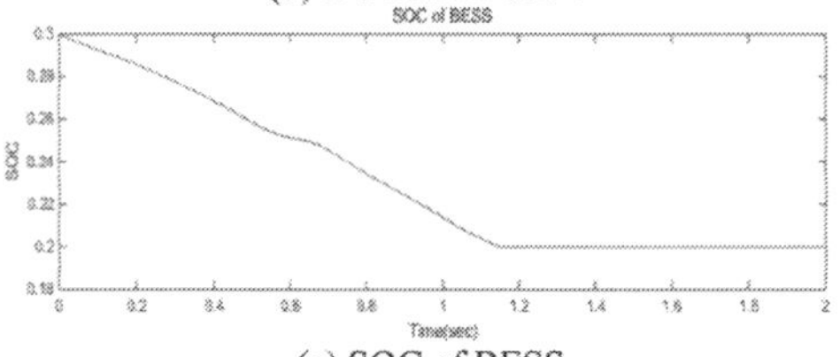

(c) SOC of BESS

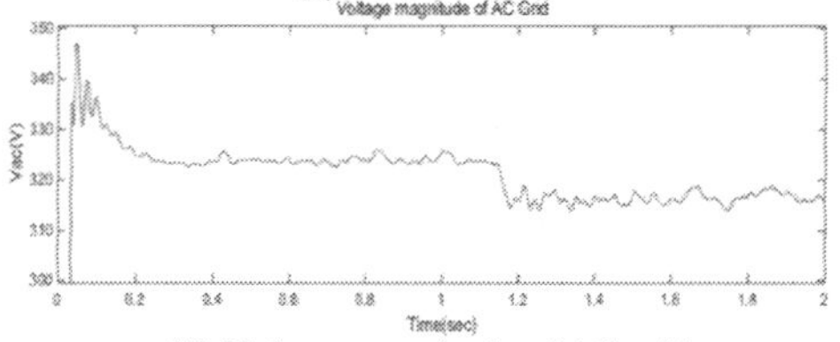

(d) Voltage magnitude of AC grid

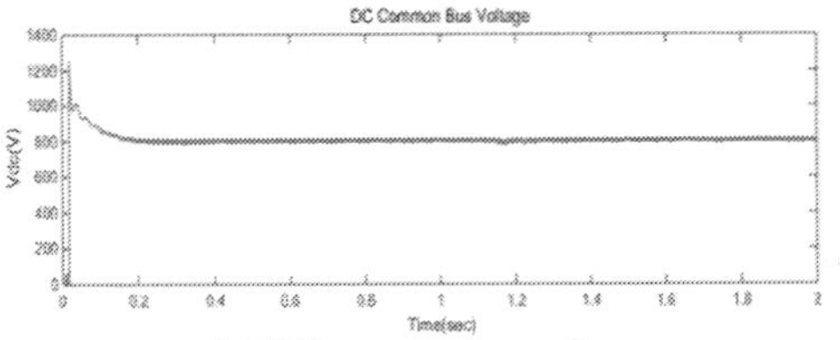

(e) DC common bus voltage

Figure 8. Simulation results without compensation scheme

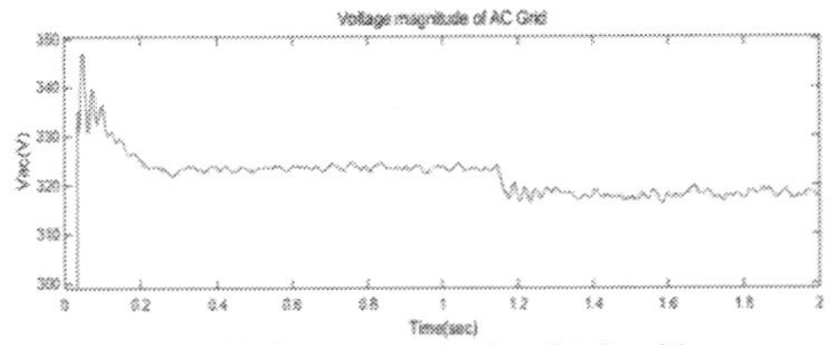

(a) Voltage magnitude of AC grid

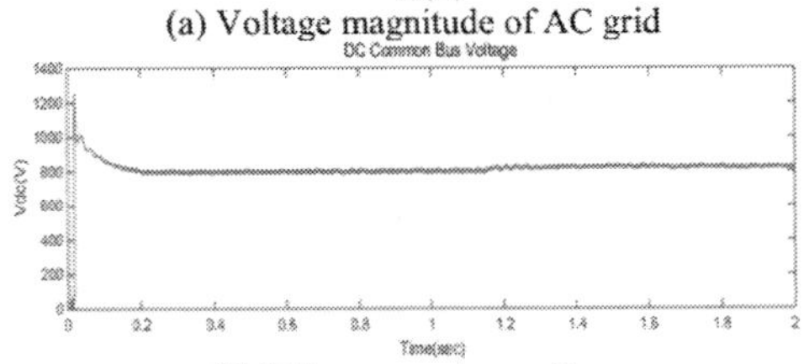

(b) DC common bus voltage

Figure 9. Simulation results with compensation scheme

Table 2. AC voltage magnitude before and after BESS is off

	Without Compensation	With Compensation
Before	323 V	323 V
After	315 V	318 V

The SOC of BESSs reaches to its minimum value at time 1.17 sec. Because of limitation, Sudden decrease of the PV-BESSs integrated system occurs. Figure 8(d) and figure 9(a) show voltage deviation which results from the sudden power decrease. In figure 8(e), DC voltage is always constant if voltage deviation occurs. In figure 9(b), DC voltage is increase because of the proposed compensation scheme. Voltage compensation scheme is validate in the simulation and proposed method can be novel and adequate method in voltage deviation.

5 Conclusion

The disadvatage of PV systems is their unstable power ouput. This unstable ouput can cause voltage instability in the LV systems. The BESSs are used for preventing the instability. However, BESSs have SOC limit in operation. If BESSs' SOC reaches its maximum or minimum value, sudden voltage deviation can occur. In this paper, DC-link voltage control to compensate the undesirable voltage deviation is proposed. Because control scheme considering SOC limit in LV networks have not been proposed, the proposed control scheme is novel. For validation of the proposed method, MATLAB/SimPowerSystems simulation tools are used. As a result of the simulation, the proposed control scheme is good for preventing voltage deviation.

References

1. D.-J. Won, Y.-S. Noh, M.-Y. Ryu, C.-Y. Won and H.-W. Lim, "A Study of Grid-connected PV-AC module with Active Power Decoupling and ESS", *2014 IEEE International Conference on Industrial Technology (ICIT)*, Feb. 26 ~ Mar. 1, 2014, Busan, Korea
2. H. Choi, M. Ciobotaru and V. G. Agelidis, "Large-Scale PV Systems with Energy Storage Utilizing High-Gain DC/DC Converters", *2014 IEEE International Conference on Industrial Technology (ICIT)*, Feb. 26 ~ Mar. 1, 2014, Busan, Korea
3. L. Zhang, et al. "Power control of DC microgrid using DC bus signaling" *Applied Power Electronics Conference and Exposition (APEC)*, 2011 Twenty-Sixth Annual IEEE. IEEE, 2011. p. 1926-1932.
4. J. J. Justo, F. Mwasilu, J. Lee and J.-W. Jang, "AC-microgrids versus DC-microgrids with distributed energy resources : A revies", *Renewable and Sustainable Energy Reviews 24*, Elsevier, 2013. p. 387-405
5. M. J. E. Alam, K. M. Muttaqi and D. Sutanto, "A Novel Approach for Ramp-Rate Control of Solar PV Using Energy Storage to Mitigate Output Fluctuations Caused by Cloud Passing", *IEEE Trans. on Energy Conversion vol. 29*. June, 2014, p. 507-518
6. F. Marra, G. Yang, C. Traeholt, J. Ostergaard and E. Larsen, "A Decentralized Storage Strategy for Residential Feeders With Photovoltaics", *IEEE Trans. on Smart Grid vol. 5*, March, 2014, p. 974-981
7. T. L. Vandoorn, B. Meersman, L. Degroote, B. Renders and L. Vandevelde, "A Control Strategy for Islanded Microgrids With DC-Link Voltage Control", *IEEE Trans. on Power Delivery vol. 26*, 2011, p. 703-713
8. H. Laaksonen, P. Saari and R. Komulainen, "Voltage and Frequency Control of Inverter Based Weak LV network Microgrid", *Future Power Systems 2005 International Conference on. IEEE*, 2005
9. G. Mokhtari, A. Ghosh, G. Nourbakhsh and G. Ledwich, "Smart Robust Resources Control in LV Network to Deal With Voltage Rise Issue", *IEEE Trans. on Sustainable Energy vol. 4*, October, 2013
10. X. J. Su, M. A. S. Masoum and P. J. Wolfs, "Optimal PV Inverter Reactive Power Control and Real Power Curtailment to Improve Performance of Unbalanced Four-Wire LV Distribution Networks", *IEEE Trans. on Sustainable Energy vol.5*, July, 2014

MATEC Web of Conferences **50**, 02002 (2016)
DOI: 10.1051/matecconf/20165002002

Energy cost saving strategies in distributed power networks

Alain Tcheukam and Hamidou Tembine

New York University Abu Dhabi, United Arab Emirates

Abstract. In this paper we study energy cost saving strategies in power networks in presence of prosumers. Three tips are considered: (i) distributed power network architecture, (ii) peak energy shaving with the integration of prosumers' contribution, (iii) Electric vehicles self-charging by means of prosumers' production. The proposed distributed power network architecture reduces significantly the transmission costs and can reduce significantly the global energy cost up to 42 percent. Different types of prosumer who use self-charging photovoltaic systems, are able to intelligently buy energy from, or sell it, to the power grid. Therein, prosumers interact in a distributed environment during the purchase or sale of electric power using a double auction with negotiation mechanism. Using a two-step combined learning and optimization scheme, each prosumer can learn its optimal bidding strategy and forecast its energy production, consumption and storage. Our simulation results, conducted for the region of Sicily in Italy, show that the integration of prosumers can reduce peak hour costs up to 19 percent and 6 percent for eligible prosumers with electric vehicles.

1 Introduction

The electric price is very cheap compared to other energy production sources. As gasoline prices increase, alternative fuels appeal more to vehicle fleet managers and consumers. The electric prices are reduced by a factor of 3.4 because electric motors are 3.4 times more efficient than internal combustion engines. Based on the US National Average Price (April 15, 2015) the electric price is $0.12/kWh is the cheapest compare to Diesel ($3.06/gallon), Natural Gas ($2.09/GGE), Propane ($2.92/gallon) and Gasoline ($2.42/gallon). Electric vehicles (EVs) use a battery to store the electric energy that powers the motor. EV batteries are charged by plugging the vehicle into an electric power source. Charging an EV through a level 2 (220 to 240 volt circuit) adds 10 to 20 miles of range per hour according to the U.S. Department of Energy (DOE) and to the National Renewable Energy Laboratory (NREL) [1]-[3].

In [4] the authors develop a strategy to coordinate the charging of autonomous plug-in electric vehicles (EVs) using a concept of non cooperative games where they force people to pay the electricity even if they do not consume. This has been done by introducing an artificial price, called local penalty cost, in other to stabilize the global system. Obviously asking to a power consumer to pay without consuming is not reasonable.

The solution we propose is that power prosumers (Figure 1) could exploit self-charging photovoltaic system for reducing the peak energy consumption and help to reduce the peak energy demand in a distributed power network.

Figure 1: Power prosumer:self-charging PV system

More specifically, we analyze the pros and cons in terms of energy cost saving for a population of electric vehicles.

The novelty of our approach is that the power prosumer combines both distributed learning and optimization to predict supply/demand and storage in a more efficient way. We use reinforcement learning to adapt prosumers price strategy at the power market and dynamic programming to predict future outcomes. We study the impact of the penetration of self-charging photovoltaic system in the Sicily region of Italy. The self-charging PV system is used by the prosumer for charging their own electric vehicles. We show through experimental studies that the population of prosumer in which there is an increasing penetration of self-charging photovoltaic system has saved the 6% of the total energy cost of the population who doesn't. The peak energy consumption has been reduced by 19%. We also show that the diversity of the power market participants (power consumers, producers and prosumers) allows to shave the peak energy consumption in the power grid.

The rest of the paper is organized as follows. In the next Section we describe the DIPONET power architecture and, the learning and optimization methods used by prosumer when buying/selling energy in the power market. In Section 3 we consider the region of Sicily (Italy) for studying the impact of self-charging photovoltaic system. Experimental and numerical results are presented in section 4. Section 5 concludes the paper. The Table 1 summarizes the notations used in the paper.

Table1: Notations

Symbol	Meaning
$[1,2,\cdots,T]$	time horizon of an entire day
Q_t	the energy profile of an entire day. $[q_1,\cdots,q_t]$
$k \in \mathbb{Z}$	maximum energy variation
$x_t \in \mathbb{Z}$	the energy variation at time t, $-k \leq x_t \leq k$.
R_{max}	maximal energy reserve capacity $R_{max} : \mathbb{N}$
R_0	initial energy reserve capacity $R_0 : \mathbb{N}$
R_t	state of the energy reserve at time t, $R_t : \mathbb{N}$
$o : \mathbb{Z} \to \mathbb{R}$	additional cost. if $0 \leq x$ then $o(x) = x$ else $x \leq o(x) \leq 0$.
$c_t : \mathbb{R}$	unitary energy cost achieved after the negotiation.
A	the strategy space of the consumer/producer
s_t	negotiation strategy at time t, $s_t \in A$
$P(t,s)$	the value of the reward associated to action s at time t.
$r(t,s)$	the reward associated to action s at time t.
$\alpha \in \mathbb{R}$	$0 < \alpha \leq 1$
$D(t)$	total demand at time t
$S(t)$	total supply at time t
n	the indice of the market participant (prosumer)
q_{mean}	average energy consumption

2 DIPONET: a grid of micro-grids

The U.S. Energy Information Administration (EIA) estimates that electricity transmission and distribution losses average about 6% of the electricity that is transmitted and distributed annually in the United States. Distributed power network architecture aims to reduce power transmission losses and to integrate renewable energy sources. We focus on the DIPONET power architecture for an efficient power grid management. The idea behind is to manage the grid as a set of micro grids and to reduce power transmission losses from the distribution systems operators to the end-users [5]-[6].

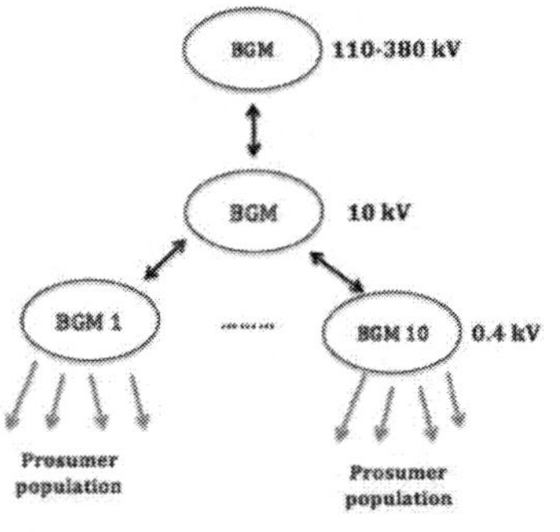

Figure 2: DIPONET power architecture.

The DIPONET architecture (Figure 2) is more dynamic and the idea is to provide the prosumer a more efficient way to interact in the distributed power network. At the power grid layer, DIPONET consists of a multi-level micro-grids architecture which is sub-divided into 4 levels. The first level (0.4 kV) is a low-range network covering subdivisions (a neighborhood). The second level (10 kV) is a medium-range area network covering a suburb (regional grid). The third level (110 kV) is a long-distance energy transport network. Finally in the fourth level (380 kV) the electricity is produced from large power plants (coal, gas or nuclear).

At the power market layer, we consider a multi-stage negotiation system through which the energy produced by micro-grids (at various tiers) are auctioned to/by the prosumers. The balancing of demand and supply between participants is carried out through balancing group managers (BGMs) which are located in different network layers and operate in parallel on each grid. The BGM balances the supply and the demand of electricity between a producer and a consumer who have submitted a similar bid.

2.1 Combined learning and optimization scheme in DIPONET

The challenge of the prosumer in DIPONET is to make elastic the demand for, and the supply of, electricity in order to optimize its energy cost based on power market conditions. Prosumer strategies are concerned with two separate phases: negotiation and optimization. We now describe the combined scheme DIPONET by means of learning [7].

Step 1: Reinforcement learning

At the end of a negotiation in the power market, the final achieved price by the prosumer, of index n, is normalized according to the frame size of the negotiation. Then, the temporal difference method [3] is used to derive the reward of the negotiation strategy currently executed.

$$P_n(t+1,s) := P_n(t,s) + \alpha\,(r_n(t,s) - P_n(t,s)); \tag{1}$$

Step 2: Optimization

The consumer is characterized by the class of energy variation profiles (s)he can adopt during the day.

Controllable inputs: we denote by the controllable input of the consumer, n at time t. The consumer has the ability to increase/decrease its energy consumption.

State of the consumer n: the state of the consumer is given by the level of the energy reserve R_{nt}

$$R_{n,t+1} = R_{nt} + q_{nt} = R_{nt} + (q_{mean} + \beta x_{nt}) \tag{2}$$

where $q_{mean}$is the average energy consumption (non shiftable energy demand), β is the consumption rate, and x_{nt} is the control action at time t.

Objective function: the objective of the consumer is to minimize the electricity cost achieved at the end of the day.

$$\min_{x_{nt}, t=1,\ldots,T} \sum_{t=1}^{T} (o(x_{nt}) + q_{nt}) * C_{nt}(D(t), S(t)) \tag{3}$$

where the energy cost C_{nt} achieved by the consumer n depends on the total energy demand and supply at time t. $o(x_{nt})$ represents the storage cost of the prosumer which depends on both the amount of electricity bought in the market and on the energy loss due to any kind of electricity transformation.

Constraints
(i) summing up all the variations from the beginning of the day to any time, we cannot exceed a lower and an upper bound of the energy reserve. This constraint accounts for available energy storage media, like electric vehicle batteries or thermic accumulations due to anticipated heating, or delayed air conditioning.

$$\forall\ 1 \le t \le T,\ 0 \le R_{n0} + \sum_{t=1}^{T} x_{nt} \le R_{n,max} \tag{4}$$

(ii) the sum of all the energy variations in the whole day for the consumer is zero, i.e. if in some slot the variation is positive, in some other slot it must be negative. $\sum_{t=1}^{T} x_{nt} = 0$

Proposed algorithm: we propose an efficient dynamic programming algorithm for planning the energy consumption/production. Each consumer n will use the algorithm to predict and control his/her energy consumption. The control algorithm of the consumer has three inputs: (i) the definition of the class of allowed profiles *Q*; and (ii) the cost of a unit of energy which is the result of the negotiation in each time step of the previous day. We denote by $C_t(D(t),S(t)) = C_t$ the achieved energy cost at time t. Hereafter, the optimization problem and the proposed dynamic programming algorithm used to solve it are defined.

Let $Z_t(Y_t) : \mathbb{R} \cup \{\infty\},\ t = 1,\ldots,T,\ 0 \le Y_t \le R_{max}$ be the optimal energy costs for time step *1,...,T* when the final energy reserve at time *t* is *Yt*. Here $Z_t(Y_t) = \infty$ if energy reserve *Yt* cannot be achieved at time step t. Thus $Z_0(Y_0)$ (no slot has elapsed yet) is everywhere ∞ except for $Z_0(R_0) = 0$

Subproblems

$$Z_t(Y_t) = \min_{x_1,\ldots,x_t} \sum_{i=1}^{t} (o(x_i) + q_i)C_i,\ t = 1,\cdots,T \tag{5}$$

$$\forall t'\ 1 \le t' \le T,\ 0 \le R_0 + \sum_{i=1}^{t'} x_i \le R_{max} \tag{6}$$

$$R_0 + \sum_{i=1}^{t} x_i = y_t \quad 0 \le y_t \le R_{max} \tag{7}$$

Dynamic programming

$$Z_t(Y_t) = \min_{\substack{-k \le x_t \le k \\ 0 \le Y_t - x_t \le R_{max}}} Z_{t-1}(Y_t - x_t) + (o(x_t) + q_t)c_t \tag{8}$$

$$Z_T(R_0) = Z \ \&\ Z_0(Y_0) = \text{ if } Y_0 = R_0 \text{ then } 0 \text{ else } \infty. \tag{9}$$

The value of *Zt* at time t is computed sequentially in terms of *Zt−1* by looking backwards for *Zt(Yt)* to the optimal energy costs at slot *t − 1* for eligible values *Yt − xt* of the energy reserve. Finally, an optimal *strategy S* is any sequence such that the values of and of are computed backwards from , *t = T* ...,1, by letting the final reserve being . Formally: optimal strategy

$$Z_t(\widehat{Y}_t) = Z_{t-1}(\widehat{y}_t - \widehat{x}_t) + (o(\widehat{x}_t) + q_t)c_t, \tag{10}$$

$$\widehat{Y_{t-1}} = \widehat{Y}_t - \widehat{x}_t,\ \widehat{Y_T} = R_0. \tag{11}$$

The time and space complexity of the algorithm are *O(T Rmax k)* and *O(T Rmax)* respectively.

3 Case study: Sicily region

In this section we consider the Sicily region of Italy. We model the cost associated to the power transmission system and the cost associated to the use of self-charging PV system by the prosumers. This cost information is used by the prosumer for predicting (optimizing) his/her future supply/demand (see Section 2 above).
The amount of electricity produced in a region trough wind turbine or solar panel depends mainly on the geographic position and of the type of the climate. In many regions and based on the time of climate, captive consumers (households and small commercial businesses) can use renewable energy sources to produce electricity that can be made available to the power grid.

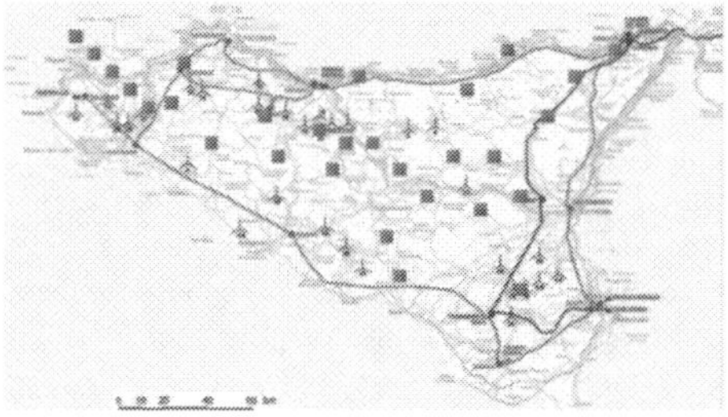

Figure 3: Sicily region: solar and wind power plants penetration

We focus our attention on the Sicily region (Figure 3) in the south of Italy which is composed of 10 regions and contents 5,092 million of habitants. In the figure, the green and red lines represent the electricity network 380−220kV in the Sicily region. The star and the square represent respectively the distribution of wind farms and solar panels in Sicily region (November 2012). In the model we study the influence of self-charging photovoltaic systems on the peak energy reduction in the power grid. In this case a part of the population, that we term prosumer, uses self-charging photovoltaic systems and do not consume additional electric power from the power grid for charging their electric vehicle. In our model, power prosumer (small businesses and households) using photovoltaic installation belongs to the first level of the DIPONET power architecture.

3.1 Cost modelling

Transmission cost modeling: electric power transmission and distribution losses include losses in transmission between sources of supply and points of distribution and in the distribution to consumers. The first step for the minimization of the energy losses is to focuses on the DIPONET architecture. The power transmission cost for a producer, consumer or prosumer, denoted by i, in a time period t is defined by the linear combination of the operational cost *Cij* in different levels j:

$$C_i(t) = \sum_{j=1}^{4} q_{ij} * r_{ij} * C_{ij}(t) \qquad (12)$$

where q is the energy injected to (or withdrawn from) the power grid and r is the rate of the energy production/consumption.

Self-charging PV cost modeling: the photovoltaic cost is given by the sum up of the technological investment (Cinvest) cost, the maintenance cost (Cmain) and the inefficiency cost (Cinef) due to the obscuration of the sunlight. The inefficiency cost depends on the dust deposition rate [2] which varies over a wide range both with respect to the time of the year and the location. The PV inefficiency cost during a time period t is then defined by:

$$C_{inef}(t) = \alpha(t) / [(s * e*) I_o \exp(-NAQ_{ext})] \qquad (13)$$

where α(t) represents the additional cost of inefficiency, s is the speciment type of the solar panel technology, e is the exposure period to the dust, N, Io is the light intensity, N is the number of deposited dust particle per unit area, A is the area occupied by a particle and *Qext* the extinction efficiency of a particle of dust (which varies from 1 to 5).

3.2 Power prosumers and electric vehicle penetrations

Based on the data of the Italian GSE, in 2012 the number of photovoltaic systems in Sicily amounted to 18,846 units with a total capacity of 836.1MW. In the model captive consumers, who are able to produce electricity through alternative energy sources, are considered power prosumer and they represent the 30% of the Sicily population. Each power prosumer owns an electrical vehicle. We study the penetration of electric vehicles in the Sicily region (Figure 3) and their impact on the overall power consumption. We consider the 10 provinces of Sicily and we model them into the DIPONET power architecture.

4 Simulations

We compare the behavior of the population in terms of energy consumption through a placebo test (Table 2). In the first case the population doesn't dispose of any self-charging PV system while in the second case they do.

Figure 4 reports the result of the placebo test of the behavior of the consumer population after one day. The dashed curve represents the amount of energy consumed in each hour by the entire population when there is no self-charging PV system in the Sicily region.

Analogously, the solid curve represents the case in which a self-charging PV system is used by 60% of the population of Sicily (nearly 3 million of persons).

The observation we have is that the consumer population when 60% (of them) makes use of the self-changing PV system has consumed less during periods when the electricity cost is high. The peak energy reduction is about 17,91% and this is a positive result for the distribution system operator.

Table 2: Experimental setup of Sicily region in the DIPONET architecture

Architecture	Negotiation Levels	3
	BGM on Level 1 ($< 0,4kV$)	10
	BGM on Level 2 ($0,4kv - 10kV$)	1
	BGM on Level 2 ($> 10kV$)	1
	Clients	
	Producers (50 – 300 KW)	
	Consumers (50 – 100 KW) in avg	
	Prosumers (50 – 300 KW) in avg	
Electricity price	Day duration: 60 slots (24 hours)	
	Profile cost of the electricity (free market)	
Prosumers environment	Prosumer with Self-charging PV	
	Population with no EV penetration	
Reserve capacity	finite	
Prosumer: controller	Combination of RL and Optimization	
	Bid strategies - Energy profiling	
Aggregator	Collection of 4 prosumers	
Simulations	Duration: 3 days - 3 months	
	Test 1: Self-charging PV penetration	
	Test 2: Peak energy shaving	

In Figure 5 the final cost achieved at the end of day 3 by the population of consumers in which the self-charging PV system was active (solid curve) is less than the case in which there was no self- charging PV system (dashed curve). The energy saving cost by the penetration of EV is about 5,33% of the energy consumes by the entire population.

We now consider the case in which the population is composed of power prosumer who do not care about the inelasticity demand constraint. We compare the behavior of the later population with the one who doesn't use DIPONET.

In Figure 6, we analyze the result of the placebo test in terms of energy cost achieved by all the population in different time of the day. We can notice that the two peaks energy consumption in the first case (dashed curve) have been anticipated in periods when the energy cost turns out to be low (solid curve). The peak remains high in the first case in which the population doesn't make use of the DIPONET optimization scheme. The analysis we make is that the system operator cannot balance such a heavy change in the consumption rate of the prosumer population. Hence, the heterogeneity of the market participant (see Figure 4) in power market indirectly helps to balance the mismatch between the energy demand and supply.

Figure 7 reports the result of the placebo test of the behavior of the consumer population after tree months. The population in the case in which there is a penetration of self-charging photovoltaic system (solid curve) has saved 19% of the total energy cost of the population who doesn't (dashed curve). The information we have is that the percentage of energy cost saving in the population keep increasing in the long run.

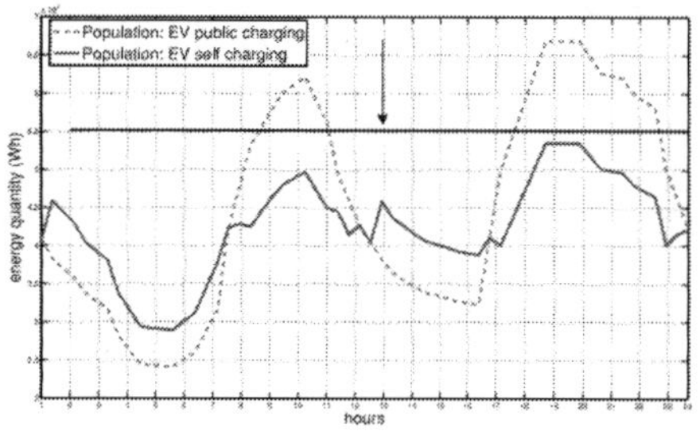

Figure 4: EV penetration: peak energy consumption shaving by 17,91 %.

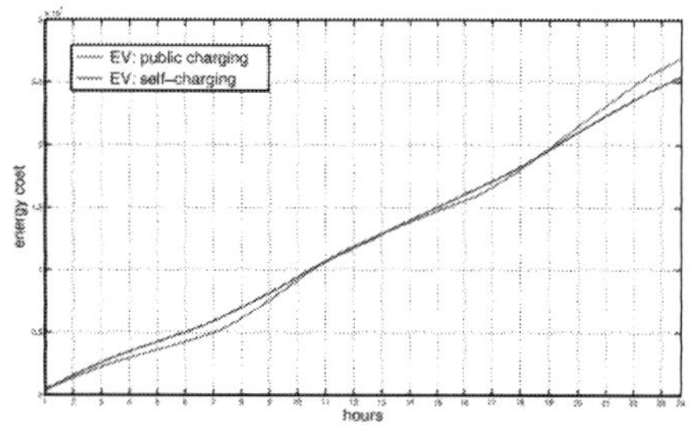

Figure 5: EV penetration: total energy cost saving about 6%

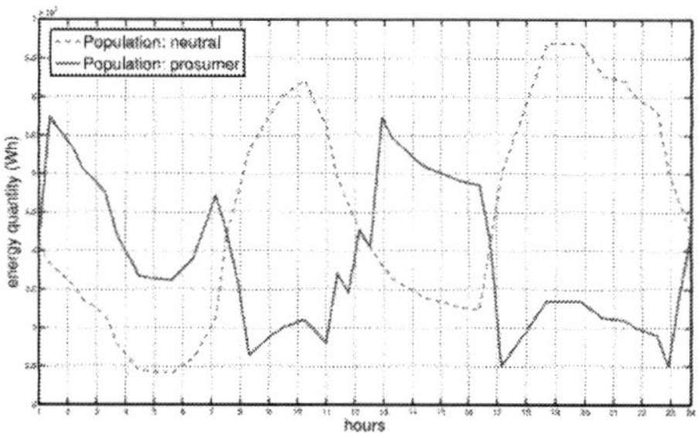

Figure 6: EV penetration 1 day duration: case of only elastic power demand.

5 Concluding remarks

This paper proposed self-charging photovoltaic system as a solution for lowering peak energy consumption by means of distributed power networks. Our study was based on the Sicily region of Italy. We have used reinforcement learning and optimization for predicting supply/demand and store energy in a more efficient way.

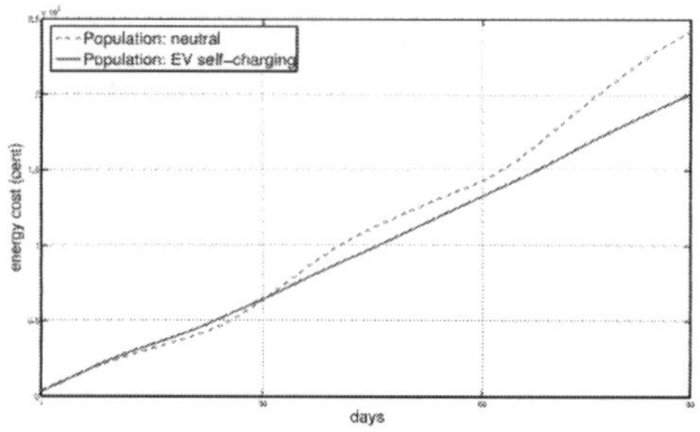

Figure 7: EV penetration 3 months duration: total energy cost saving about 19%.

References

1. M. Balijepalli and K. Pradhan, "Review of Demand Response under Smart Grid Paradigm". IEEE PES Innovative Smart Grid Tech- nologies, (2011).
2. M. Mazumder, *et al*; "Characterization of electrodynamic screen performance for dust removal from solar panels and solar hydrogen generators". IEEE Industry Applications Society Annual Meeting (IAS), (2011).
3. R. Sutton, A. Barto, and C. Anderson, Reinforcement Learning: An Introduction, The MIT Press, 1983.
4. Z. Ma, D. Callaway and I. Hiskens, "Decentralized charging control for large populations of plug-in vehicles, " in Proc. Conference on Decision and Control, pp. 206-212 , (2010).
5. U. Montanari, A. T. Siwe, Real time market models and prosumer profiling. IEEE Conference on Computer Communication Workshop, pages 712, (2013).
6. U. Montanari, A. T. Siwe, Prosumers as Aggregators in the DEZENT Context of Regenerative Power Production IEEE International Conference on Self-Adaptive and Self-Organizing Systems (SASO), pp. 167- 174, (2014).
7. H. Tembine, Distributed strategic learning for wireless engineers, CRC Press, Taylor & Francis Inc,(2012).

MATEC Web of Conferences **50**, 02003 (2016)
DOI: 10.1051/matecconf/20165002003

Mechanical Calculation of Power Lines and Strands in Overhead Transmission Lines

Yongping Li[1], Yu Liu[2] and Jibin Zhang[3]

[1] Computational Mechanics, Northeast Dianli University, 132012 Jilin, China
[2] Civil Engineering, Northeast Dianli University, 132012 Jilin, China
[3] Transmission Engineering, Northeast Dianli University, 132012 Jilin, China

Abstract. This paper discusses the issue of shape and stress of overhead transmission lines. It fully considers that the conductor is subjected to axial force, shear, bending moment simultaneousiy. And the flat wire is basically in the elastic range. Because the stress is the strength of a certain point, the bending rigidity of the overhead lines can not be ignored. However, the catenary has been used in previous research and the force of the overhead lines is obtained on this basis. The author establishes a model of wire calculation under real condition, and gives a feasible simplified model. And then it gives the line shape formula, internal force formula, formula of stress in the strands. The results show that the original stress is significantly smaller.In this paper, the stress formula is almost close to the reality. It proves the reliability of the simplified model that the line shape includes the original flexible part.The results can not only fill the gaps in the theoretical study of the overhead lines, but also have some guidance to the production and design of overhead lines.

1 Introduction

So far the hypothesis has been adopted in the study of wire mechanics that line shape of overhead transmission line is catenary [1-5]. The conductor is only subjected to axial force, and the stress of the wire is replaced by the average stress. The average stress is equal to the axial force divided by the cross-sectional area of the wire. However, the real line shape of the hanging wire is not catenary. The real wire is rigid and it is subjected to axial force, shear force and bending moment unlike a cable that is just under tension. The previous hypothesis leads to the stress of the conductor far away from the actual stress, so that there are hidden dangers in the strength design. The purpose of this paper is to study the wire alignment under the natural suspended state, and the axial force, shear force and bending moment of the conductor under this condition. Next, the author obtains the line shape from the static equilibrium analysis, and thus finds out the internal force of the wire and the stress of the strands.

2 Overhead line alignment

Assume that the wire is regarded as a soft line in deformation due to excessive span. The assumption can simplify the analysis and calculation. And the catenary formula under this assumption [6] is easy to remember. Because the stress is the force received on the unit area, the bending rigidity of the overhead transmission lines is not small even in a very small wire. So bending stress should not be ignored.

2.1 Alignment analysis

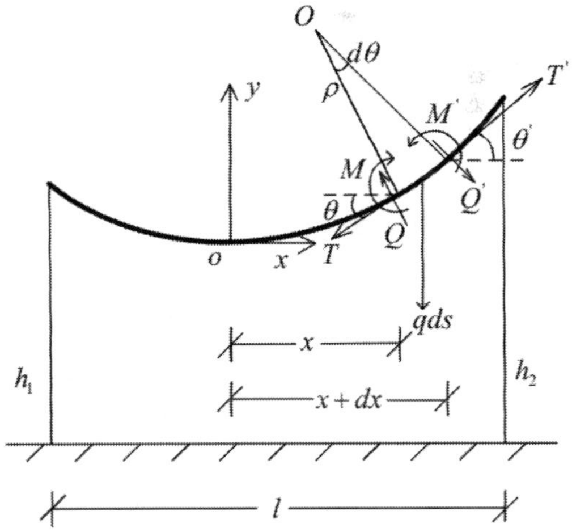

Figure 1. Natural hanging state diagram of wire in single span. Schematic diagram of force analysis of conductor.

Figure 1 shows the natural state of single span wire in suspension. Select any wire element for mechanical analysis. The static equilibrium equations of the selected element are as follows.

$$\begin{cases} T'\cos\theta' - T\cos\theta + Q'\sin\theta' - Q\sin\theta = 0 \\ T'\sin\theta' - T\sin\theta - Q'\cos\theta' + Q\cos\theta - qds = 0 \\ M' - M + T\sin\theta dx - T\cos\theta dy - qds\dfrac{dx}{2} = 0 \end{cases} \quad (1)$$

$$\begin{cases} \dfrac{dM}{ds} = Q \\ \dfrac{dQ}{ds} = \dfrac{T}{\rho} - q\cos\theta \\ \dfrac{dT}{ds} = q\sin\theta - \dfrac{Q}{\rho} \end{cases} \quad (2)$$

$$\frac{d\rho}{ds}\frac{d^2M}{ds^2} + \rho\frac{d^3M}{ds^3} + \frac{d\rho}{ds}q\cos\theta + \frac{1}{\rho}\frac{dM}{ds} - q\sin\theta = 0 \quad (3)$$

The differential relationship of moment, shear and axial force can be calculated by the formula (1). The formula (3) is obtained by the equation group (2). And the formula (3) is the static equilibrium line of the overhead lines considering the moment, shear and axial force. Because too complicated and difficult to solve, it is necessary to be simplified.

2.2 Simplified alignment

For most of the plain, the wire is relatively flat. It is considered within the elastic range. So the bending moment and curvature has the following relations in the formula (4) [7,8].

$$\frac{1}{\rho} = \frac{M}{EI} \quad (4)$$

$$\frac{d^3\rho}{d\theta^3} - \frac{9}{\rho}\frac{d\rho}{d\theta}\frac{d^2\rho}{d\theta^2} + \frac{12}{\rho^2}\left(\frac{d\rho}{d\theta}\right)^3 + \frac{d\rho}{d\theta} - a^3\rho^3\cos\theta\frac{d\rho}{d\theta} + 2a^3\rho^4\sin\theta = 0 \quad (5)$$

Formula (5) was obtained by formula (4) into the formula (3). The formula (5) is a three order's, nonlinear, variable coefficient's and non-homogeneous equation. The equation's analytical solution is difficult to be obtained.

Because the wire is flat, its curvature radius changes very slowly along with the dip angle. Thus the ones are very small relative to the rest .They can be ignored that the two order derivative,third order derivative and the cubic of the first derivative of curvature radius and dip angle. And the corresponding coefficient is smaller than 1. Ignore them and retain the main items. Simplified model is obtained by (6-1) or (6-2).

$$\frac{d\rho}{d\theta} - a^3\rho^3\cos\theta\frac{d\rho}{d\theta} + 2a^3\rho^4\sin\theta = 0 \quad (6\text{-}1)$$

$$\frac{d\rho}{d\theta} = \frac{2a^3\rho^4\sin\theta}{a^3\rho^3\cos\theta - 1} \quad (6\text{-}2)$$

$$a^3 = \frac{q}{EI} \quad (6\text{-}3)$$

This is a first order's, nonlinear, variable coefficient's and non-homogeneous equation. Its analytical solution is (7).

$$\cos\theta = \sqrt{\frac{\rho_0}{\rho}}\left(1 + \frac{1}{5a^3\rho^3}\right) - \frac{1}{5a^3\rho^3} \quad (7)$$

The formula (7) is the exact result of the simplified model. It is also the linear analytical solution. Although it is an implicit equation, it is one of the important results of this research. And it is so far unique result.

It is not difficult to prove that the first part of formula (7) is on behalf of the catenary, the second part is a correction term due to the influence of the shear and bending moment. Formula (7) contains the catenary, reflecting the rule that general contains special. It illustrates the rationality, scientificalness and credibility of the simplified method for the formula (3).

2.3 Determining the phenotype of alignment

Explicit formula of formula (7) is determined as follows.

$$\rho = \rho_0 + \Delta\rho,$$

$$\frac{1}{\rho} = \frac{y''}{\left(1 + y'^2\right)^{3/2}},$$

Because the $\dfrac{\Delta\rho}{\rho_0}$ is very small, the formula (8) is obtained.

$$\begin{cases} x = \dfrac{a^3\rho_0^4}{1 - a^3\rho_0^3}\left[\theta + \sin\theta\cos\theta - \left(3 - \dfrac{1}{a^3\rho_0^3}\right)\sin\theta\right] \\ y = \dfrac{a^3\rho_0^4}{1 - a^3\rho_0^3}\left[\theta + \sin^2\theta - (1 - \cos\theta)\left(3 - \dfrac{1}{a^3\rho_0^3}\right)\right] \end{cases} \quad (8)$$

Formula (8) is an explicit equation of overhead lines in general. Its coordinate system is shown in Figure 1. The lowest point of the wire is the origin. The right is the X axis and the up is the Y axis. The formula (8) is a parameter equation of ρ_0 and θ. ρ_0 is the curvature radius of the lowest point of the overhead line. θ is the angle between the tangent direction and the horizontal direction of the wire.

3 Mechanical calculation of overhead line

3.1 Internal force calculation of overhead line

By formula (7), ρ_0 can be found in the determination of θ. By the radius of curvature ρ, the internal force can be obtained under the assumption of elasticity.

1） moment,

$$M = \frac{EI}{\rho} \quad (9)$$

2） shear,

$$Q = \frac{2EI\rho q \sin\theta}{EI - q\rho^3 \cos\theta} \quad (10)$$

3）axial force,

$$T = \rho\frac{dQ}{ds} + \rho q\cos\theta = \frac{dQ}{d\theta} + \rho q\cos\theta \quad (11\text{-}1)$$

$$T = \rho q\cos\theta + 2\rho q\frac{(a^3\rho^3 - 1)(\cos\theta - a^3\rho^3) + 2a^3\rho^3\sin^2\theta(1 + 2a^3\rho^3\cos\theta)}{(a^3\rho^3\cos\theta - 1)^3} \quad (11\text{-}2)$$

At the lowest point of the wire ($\theta = 0$), its axial force is seen in the formula (11-3).

$$T_0 = \rho_0 q + \frac{2\rho_0 q}{a^3\rho^3 - 1} = \rho_0 q(1 - \frac{2}{a^3\rho^3 - 1}) \quad (11\text{-}3)$$

The former represents the axial force of the span wire. The latter is an additional term due to the influence of bending moment and shear. It is proved that the true axial force of the wire is lower than that of the flexible wire.

Table 1. Internal force table

	auther
Axial force (N)	21463
Shear force (N)	0.000165
Bending moment (N•mm)	771.82

Numerical value in table 1 is obtained by the wire of LGJ400/35 in elevation suspension state. Assumed that the span is equal to 545m and the sag is equal to 23m. The internal force is obtained at the point where $\theta = 10°$. The cross section of LGJ400/35 is shown in Figure 2. Parameters of LGJ400/35 are shown in Table 2.

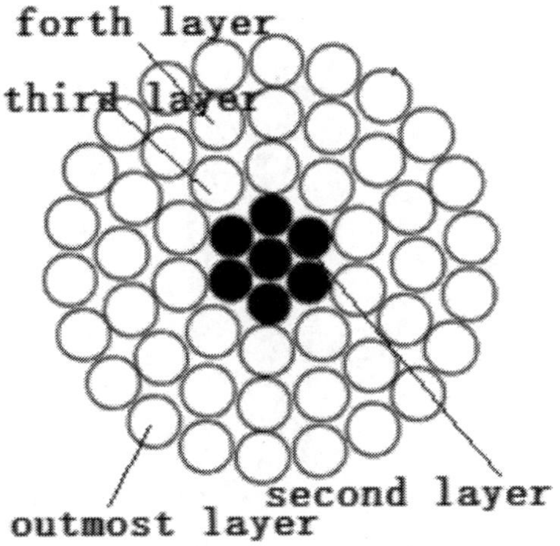

Figure 2. Cross section of LGJ400/35.

Table 2. Parameters of LGJ400/35..

d_s(mm)	d_a(mm)	E_s(N/mm^2)	E_a(N/mm^2)
2.50	3.22	202000	68000

d_s is diameter of steel core and d_a is diameter of aluminum strand.

3.2 Stress of strand calculation of overhead line

The premise of wire breaking is the strands breaks.And the first break of the strands is the outermost strand. So this paper analyzes the axial normal stress of the most outer strand. The axial normal stress is normal referred to as the strand stress. It is obvious that there are two kinds of stresses. One is caused by the axial tension of the wire. The other is caused by the bending of the wire. The total stress of the strands is $\sigma = \sigma_l + \sigma_M$, not the empirical formula $\sigma_1 = \frac{T}{A}$ [1].

3.2.1 The stress of the strand caused by the axial tension of the wire

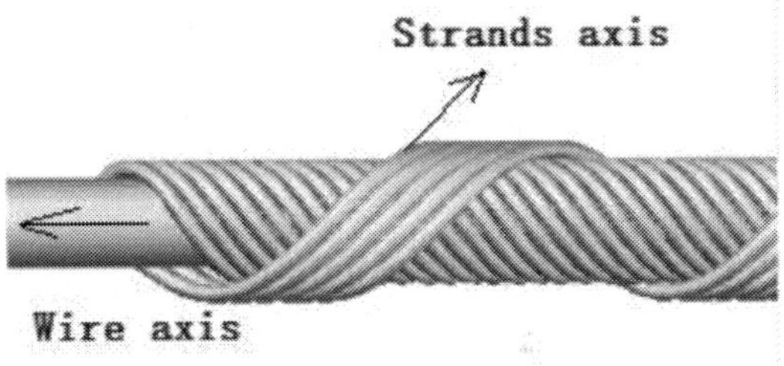

Figure 3. Diagram of the wire axis and the srrands axis.

The strain of the strand is along the direction of the strand, not the axial direction of the wire. The outermost strand stress is showed in formula (12).

$$\sigma_l = E_a\varepsilon_l = E_a(\cos^2\alpha_n - \mu_n\sin^2\alpha_n)\varepsilon_u \quad (12)$$

$$\varepsilon_u = \frac{T}{EA} \quad (13)$$

E_a is the elastic modulus of the aluminum strand. ε_l is the axial strain of the strands and ε_u is the axial strain of the wire. α_n is the winding angle of strands. μ_n is the Poisson's ratio of the wire and it can be regarded as equal to μ [9]. T is the axial tension of the wire and EA is the tensile stiffness of the conductor section.

$$\sigma_l = \frac{TE_a}{EA}(\cos^2\alpha_n - \mu_n \sin^2\alpha_n) \quad (14)$$

3.2.2 The stress of the strand caused by wire bending

The bending of a wire is an objective existence. There is a formula (4) in the elastic range. So section normal stress is as follows.

$$\sigma'_M = \frac{Ey}{\rho} = \frac{E_a M(D-d_n)}{2EI} \quad (15)$$

E_a is the elastic modulus of the aluminum strand. dn is the diameter of the aluminum strand. M is the bending moment of the wire. D is diameter of conductor section and EI is bending rigidity of conductor section.

Considering the angle between the wire axis and the strand, the stress in the strand is showed in formula (16).

$$\sigma_M = \frac{E_a M(D-d_n)}{2EI}(\cos^2\alpha_n - \mu_n \sin^2\alpha_n) \quad (16)$$

3.2.3 The total stress of the strand by the superposition of the two stresses

$$\sigma = \sigma_l + \sigma_M = E_a[\frac{T}{EA} + \frac{M(D-d_n)}{2EI}](\cos^2\alpha_n - \mu_n \sin^2\alpha_n) \quad (17)$$

It is obvious that the stress caused by stretching and bending is greater than one received tension only . The growth rate is e. EI and EA are respectively representing the tensile stiffness and the flexural rigidity of the cross section [10].

Table 3. Stress of strands.

Outermost layer (N/mm)	134.26
Forth layer (N/mm)	45.30
Third layer (N/mm)	45.35
Second layer (N/mm)	45.39

The basic assumption of the table 3 is the same as 3.1 .

$$e = \frac{M(D-d_n)}{2EI} \cdot \frac{EA}{T} \times 100\% \quad (18\text{-}1)$$

Because $MT \approx EIq$ at the lowest point in the wire, the ratio is showed as follows.

$$e = \frac{q(D-d_n)}{2T^2} \cdot EA \times 100\% \quad (18\text{-}2)$$

The error rate is not negligible because it is generally more than 20%. It can reach 35% or even higher in the large cross-section wire. However, the flexible conductor just ignores the bending stress.

Moreover there is no formula of stress in the catenary. Occasionally it is replaced by the stress of the rod. That is not scientific. Because the elastic modulus of steel strands is almost 3 times higher than the elastic modulus of aluminum strands. Stress is the force of a certain point, and it must be respectively calculated either the stresses of the steel strands or the aluminum strands. Otherwise the error is very large.

4 Conclusion

In this paper, explicit and implicit linear formulas of the overhead lines are obtained by using the method of differential calculus and elastic mechanics. The linear formula is derived by taking into account that the conductor is subjected to bending moment, shear force and axial force simultaneously. And on this basis, the paper carries out the analysis of the internal force of the wire, the analysis of the stress of the strands and the calculation of the conductor sag. Finally they are truly expressed, that the linear, stress and sag in the natural state of suspension. This paper not only makes up the theoretical gaps in the field of the mechanical calculation of wire, but also provides the modeling basis and the analysis method for the research of the related problems. It has a certain guiding significance for transmission line construction, but also provides a theoretical basis for the design and production of wires.

References

1. S.-M.. Meng, Wei. Kong, *Overhead transmission line design* (China Electric Power Press, China Beijing, 2007)
2. D.-S. Zhang, *Design Handbook for high voltage power supply circuit of electric power engineering* (China Electric Power Press, China Beijing, 2004)
3. B.-Z. Li, *High voltage overhead power transmission line construction calculation principle* (China Electric Power Press, China Beijing, 2008)
4. G.-Z. Jiang, China. Science Technology and Engineering **8**, 8 (2008)
5. X. Wei, S.-Z.. Qiang, China. Building Science Research of Sichuan **29**, 4 (2003)
6. W.-H. Zhang, J.-B. Yu, China. Electric Power Construction **33**, 2 (2012)
7. X.-F. Sun, X.-Y. Fang, L.-T. Guan, *mechanics of materials* (Higher Education Press, China Beijing, 2006)
8. S. P. Timoshenko, *mechanics of materials* (Sciencec Press, China Beijing, 1978)
9. Y.-P. Li, X.-F. Yun, W.-J. Li, China. Electric Power Construction **10**, 10 (1999)
10. Y.-P. Li, Z.-Y. Huang, Y. Ni, China. Water Resources and Power **30**, 2 (2012)

MATEC Web of Conferences **50**, 02004 (2016)
DOI: 10.1051/matecconf/20165002004

A Simple Short Circuit Analysis for Power Networks

İlhan Koşalay

Ankara Univ, Faculty of Engineering, Electrical and Electronics Engineering Department Ankara, Turkey

Abstract. This study investigates the transient behavior of short circuits in power circuits. The circuit consists of two part; input part and load part. These two parts are connected with a circuit breaker switch. The circuit works in two modes; first mode is when the switch is open and second mode is when the switch is closed. This study analyses the circuit when the switch is closed. The analysis is done with different types of closing angle. The analysis is done by forming state equations and those equations are solved numerically by using Matlab. The analysis and conclusion is performed by observing the behaviors of the graphs.

1 Introduction

Closing operation of a transmission line or a inductive / capacitive circuit can produce transient overvoltage's due to several factors. One of the most important factors, that have more influence on the peak value of voltage, can be assumed as the instant of closing [1]. For the transmission lines, the transient over voltages due to the switching of circuit are limited because of pre insertion resistors in the line circuit breakers [2, 3]. On the other side, using controlled closing can effectively limit the overvoltages and eliminate the need for closing resistors [4]. For an ideal condition, the circuit breaker (CB) contacts should touch completely when the voltage over the contacts is zero. But in real applications, the CB operating time may change. The variation of closing time of the CB contacts is assumed to change as a Gaussian distribution [5]. The value of the rate of decrease of dielectric strength should exceed the maximum derivative of the applied voltage for proper operation of CB. The maximum pre-striking voltage is determined according to the statistical scatter of the contact's speed [6].

The purpose of this paper is to create a simple and effective tool for investigation voltage changes due to the closing operations. The newly developed tool for closing transients is in good agreement with the practical applications. Inductive / capacitive circuit transient over voltages were examined in [7]. In this paper, a simulation analysis based on state equations is presented to find the closing transient over voltages and the other possible voltage variations due to the short circuits.

2 State Model For The Single Phase Switch Opening And Closing

Figure 1 shows and proposes a circuit model for switching analysis for the power circuits.

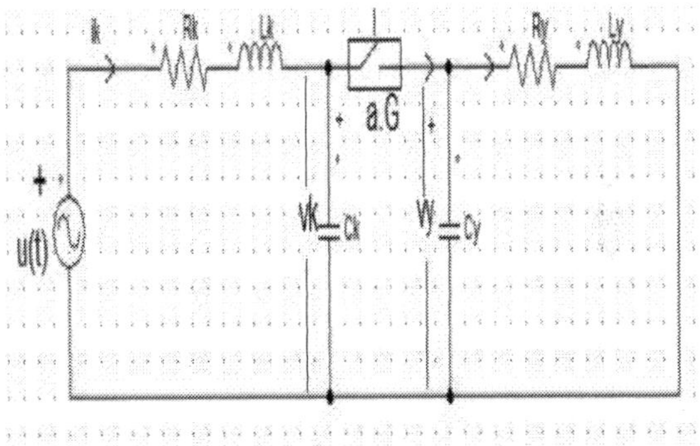

Figure 1. A proposed switching transient investigation model

If the switch is open a=0; a.G =0 and it means no conductivity. When the switch is closed a=1; a.G is very large, it means that circuit is closed. Source voltage is assumed pure sinus signal as $U(t)=\sqrt{2}\,V.\sin(\omega t + \theta)$

State model of the system is derived the circuit which is shown in figure1 and they are given in below,

$$L_k.\frac{di_k}{dt} = -R_k i_k - v_k - u(t) \qquad (1)$$

$$C_k.\frac{dv_k}{dt} = i_k - a.G(v_k - v_y) \qquad (2)$$

$$L_y.\frac{di_y}{dt} = -R_y i_y + v_y \qquad (3)$$

$$C_y.\frac{dv_y}{dt} = a.G\,(v_k - v_y) - i_y \qquad (4)$$

As a result, state equations can be summarized as below,

$$\frac{d}{dt}\begin{bmatrix} i_k \\ v_k \\ i_y \\ v_y \end{bmatrix} = \begin{bmatrix} -\frac{R_k}{L_k} & -\frac{1}{L_k} & 0 & 0 \\ \frac{1}{C_k} & -\frac{a.G}{C_k} & 0 & \frac{a.G}{C_k} \\ 0 & 0 & -\frac{R_y}{L_y} & \frac{1}{L_y} \\ 0 & \frac{a.G}{C_y} & -\frac{1}{C_y} & -\frac{a.G}{C_y} \end{bmatrix} \begin{bmatrix} i_k \\ v_k \\ i_y \\ v_y \end{bmatrix} + \begin{bmatrix} -\frac{1}{L_k} \\ 0 \\ 0 \\ 0 \end{bmatrix} u(t)$$
(5)

Output magnitudes of the system are mentioned in equation (2.6). Here; i_A : Current passing through the switch and u_T : Recovery voltage

$$\begin{bmatrix} i_A \\ u_T \end{bmatrix} = \begin{bmatrix} 0 & a.G & 0 & -a.G \\ 0 & 1 & 0 & -1 \end{bmatrix} \begin{bmatrix} i_k \\ v_k \\ i_y \\ v_y \end{bmatrix} \quad (6)$$

When the switch is closed a=1 a.G: Very large,
$u_k = v_y$; $\frac{dv_k}{dt} = \frac{dv_y}{dt}$

In this situation both u_k and v_y can not be state variables at the same time. If we v_y is chosen as a state variable equation (2.2) and 2.(4) can be written as shown below:

$$C_k \cdot \frac{dv_y}{dt} = i_k \quad (7)$$

$$C_y \cdot \frac{dv_y}{dt} = i_y \quad (8)$$

Adding equation (7) and (8) gives;

$$(C_k + C_y) \cdot \frac{dv_y}{dt} = i_k - i_y \quad (9)$$

$$\frac{dv_y}{dt} = \frac{1}{C_k+C_y} i_k - \frac{1}{C_k+C_y} i_y \quad (10)$$

For the closed switch condition, state equations become as below:

$$\frac{d}{dt}\begin{bmatrix} i_k \\ i_y \\ v_y \end{bmatrix} = \begin{bmatrix} -\frac{R_k}{L_k} & 0 & -\frac{1}{L_k} \\ 0 & -\frac{R_y}{L_y} & \frac{1}{L_y} \\ \frac{1}{C_k+C_y} & \frac{1}{C_k+C_y} & 0 \end{bmatrix} \begin{bmatrix} i_k \\ i_y \\ v_y \end{bmatrix} + \begin{bmatrix} -\frac{1}{L_k} \\ 0 \\ 0 \end{bmatrix} u(t)$$
(11)

$$i_A = \begin{bmatrix} \frac{C_y}{C_k+C_y} & \frac{C_k}{C_k+C_y} & 0 \end{bmatrix} \begin{bmatrix} i_k \\ i_y \\ v_y \end{bmatrix} \quad (12)$$

When the switch is closed, it can be investigated the below transient events using equation (11) and (12):

a) Energization of large inductive load: C_k and C_y are negligible
b) Energization of large capacitive load: R_y and L_y are negligible.
c) Short circuit current: $R_y = 0$; C_k, C_y and L_y are negligible.

From special cases a, b, and c above first or second order differential equation is obtained and analytical solution of the equation can be found. Since the circuit was operating in continuous in sinusoidal mode before the switch was closed, in the investigation of transient events when the switch is closed initial conditions is obtained as follows (Here, θ: Respective angle when the switch is closed.).

$$|Z_k| = \sqrt{R_k^2 + (\omega L_k - \frac{1}{\omega C_k})^2}; \quad \alpha = \tan^{-1}(\frac{\omega^2 L_k C_k - 1}{\omega R_k C_k}) ;$$
(13)

$$i_k(0) = \frac{\sqrt{2}V}{|Z_k|}\sin(\theta - \alpha) \quad (14)$$

$$v_k(0) = \frac{\sqrt{2}V}{\omega C_k |Z_k|}\sin(\theta - \alpha - 90°) = v_y(0) \quad (15)$$

$$i_y(0) = 0 \quad (16)$$

A graphical based interface is created in MATLAB environment is shown in figure 2.

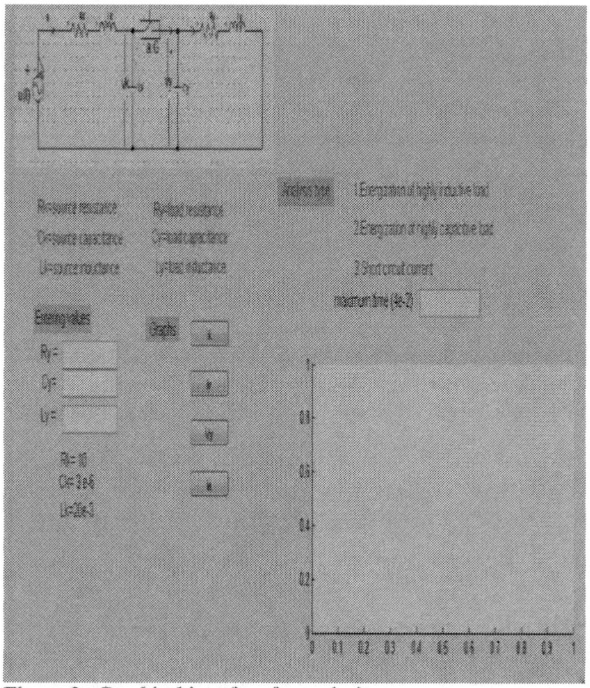

Figure 2. Graphical interface for analysis.

3 Analysis of Short Circuit

Short circuit is analyzed by letting the value of load resistance Ry=0 with large value of Cy (0.001 F)

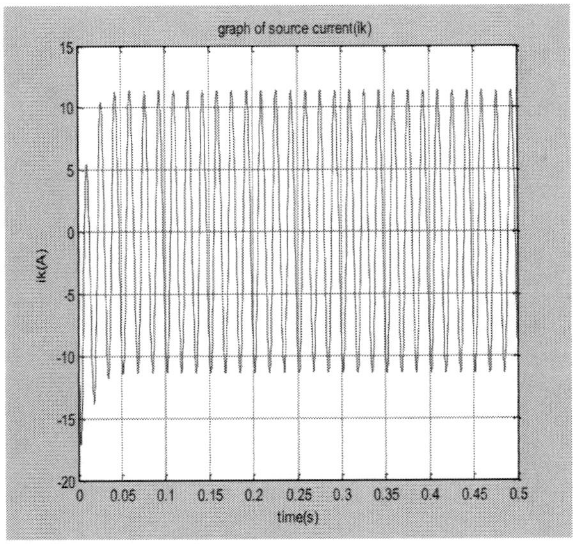

Figure 3. Graph of the source current during energization of short circuited load for $\theta = \pi/2$.

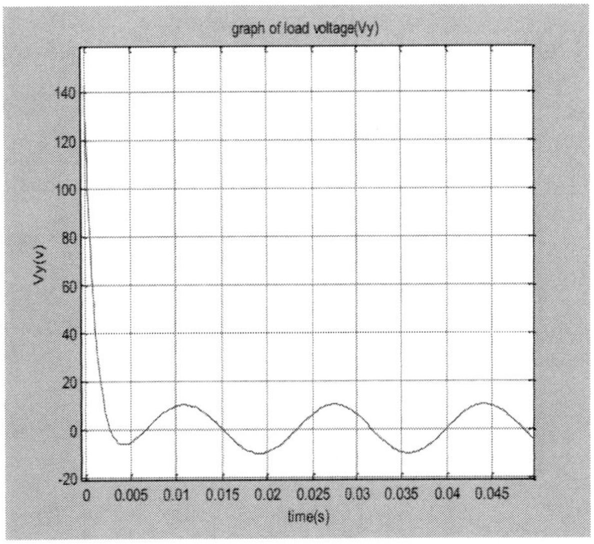

Figure 5. Graph of the load voltage during energization of short circuited load for $\theta = \pi/2$

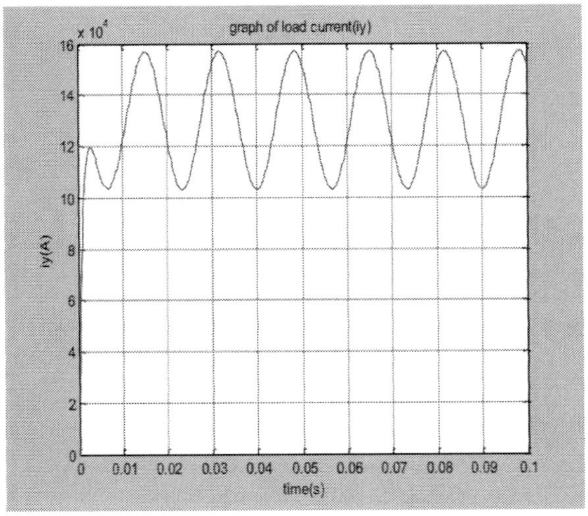

Figure 4. graph of the load current during energization of short circuited load for $\theta = \pi/2$.

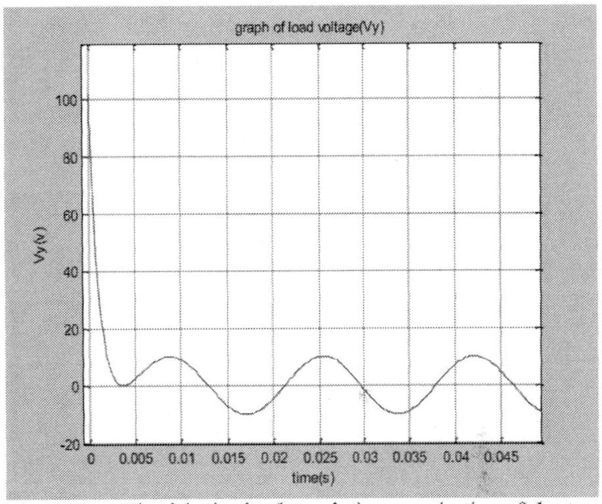

Figure 6. graph of the load voltage during energization of short circuited load for $\theta = 3\pi/4$.

Figure 3-6 show different outputs related to short circuit condition respectively. All values of θ makes the load to show transient behavior at the beginning, but for different values the level at which current attains steady state is different. Small values of θ causes the current to reach its steady state at lower values while $\theta = \pi/2$ gives the highest level.

The time spent before reaching state is same for different values of θ, for the graphs above it shows that every graph reaches its steady state at 0.01 second.

The load voltage starts at its initial value and falls rapidly. After some times it attains its steady state, for different values of θ the steady state peak value is same but the initial values are different. Value $\theta = \pi/2$ gives the highest initial value.

4 Conclusions

When the short circuit occurs in power networks, the short circuit makes the load to show transient behavior. The transient behaviors are different for different types of loads. Depending on values of angle when the circuit is closed (θ), transient time can be short or long. During transient periods, overvoltage occurs most of the time. To analyze and examine this kind of overvoltage is not easy every time due to complex parameters. This study analyzed closing transients in case of short circuit.

References

1. J. A. Martinez-Velasco, *Power System Transients, Parameter Determination*. Boca Raton, FL: CRC, Taylor & Francis Group, 2010.
2. P. Mestas and M. C. Tavares, "Comparative analysis of control switching transient techniques in transmission lines energization maneuver," presented at the Int. Conf. Power Syst. Transients, Lyon, France, Jun. 4–7, 2007.
3. M. Sanaye-Pasand, M. R. Dadashzadeh, and M. Khodayar, "Limitation of transmission line switching overvoltages using switchsync relays," presented at the Int. Conf. Power Syst. Transients, Montreal, QC, Canada, Jun. 19–23, 2005.
4. K. M. C. Dantas,D. Jr. Fernandes, W. L. A. Neves, B. A. Souza, and L. C. A. Fonseca, "Mitigation of switching overvoltages in transmission lines via controlled switching," presented at the IEEE Power Energy Soc. Gen. Meeting, Pittsburgh, PA, Jul. 20–24, 2008.
5. U. Samitz, H. Siguerdidjane, F. Boudaoud, P. Bastard, J. P. Dupraz,M. Collet, J.Martin, and T. Jung, "On controlled switching of high voltage unloaded transmission lines," in *Proc. Elektrotech. Inf.*, Paris, France, Aug. 2002, vol. 119, no. 12, pp. 415–421.
6. K. Frohlish, C. Hoelzl, M. Stanek, A. C. Carvalho, W. Hofbauer, P. Hoegg, B. L. Avent, D. F. Peelo, and J. H. Sawada, "Controlled closing on shunt reactor compensated transmission lines part I: Closing control device development," *IEEE Trans. Power Del.*, vol. 12, no. 2, pp.734–740, Apr. 1997.
7. MBONDE Shaban, KOŞALAY İlhan, "State equation based closing simulation", Communications, Series A2-A3Physics, vol: 57, number: 2 , page: 013-023 , ISSN: 1303-6009, 2015

AUTHOR INDEX

Chang Jae-won 22
Chen Peng 10
Fuangpian Phanupong 17
Hu Xiaoqing 10
Ji Wenlu 10
Kheldoun A. 1
Kim Yun-su 22
Kosalay Ilhan 35
Lee Gyu-sub 22
Li Bo 6
Li Yongping 31
Liu Yu 31
Madi S. 1
Moon Seung-il 22
Ruankorn Sayan 17
Shen Peifeng 10
Suwanasri Thanapong 17
Tang Hengxian 6
Tcheukam Alain 26
Tembine Hamidou 26
Wang Beibei 10
Wang Liang 6
Zafar Taimoor 17
Zhang Jibin 31

EDP Sciences – Web of Conferences
17, Avenue du Hoggar
Parc d'Activité de Courtabouf
BP 112
F-91944 Les Ulis Cedex A
France

ISBN 978-1-5108-2214-6

CURRAN ASSOCIATES INC.
proceedings.com